INTRODUCING
ISSUES WITH
OPPOSING
VIEWPOINTS®

# Gay Marriage

Lauri S. Scherer, *Book Editor*

**GREENHAVEN PRESS**
*A part of Gale, Cengage Learning*

GALE
CENGAGE Learning·

Farmington Hills, Mich • San Francisco • New York • Waterville, Maine
Meriden, Conn • Mason, Ohio • Chicago

Elizabeth Des Chenes, *Director, Content Strategy*
Douglas Dentino, *Manager, New Product*

*For more information, contact:*
Greenhaven Press
27500 Drake Rd.
Farmington Hills, MI 48331-3535
Or you can visit our Internet site at gale.cengage.com

For product information and technology assistance, contact us at

Gale Customer Support, 1-800-877-4253
For permission to use material from this text or product, submit all requests online at
www.cengage.com/permissions

Further permissions questions can be e-mailed to permissionrequest@cengage.com

Articles in Greenhaven Press anthologies are often edited for length to meet page require-ments. In addition, original titles of these works are changed to clearly present the main thesis and to explicitly indicate the author's opinion. Every effort is made to ensure that Greenhaven Press accurately reflects the original intent of the authors. Every effort has been made to trace the owners of copyrighted material.

Cover image © Laurin Rinder/Shutterstock.com.

**LIBRARY OF CONGRESS CATALOGING-IN-PUBLICATION DATA**

Gay marriage / Lauri S. Scherer, book editor.
      pages cm. -- (Introducing issues with opposing viewpoints)
   Includes bibliographical references and index.
   ISBN 978-0-7377-6923-4 (hardcover)
   1. Same-sex marriage--United States--Juvenile literature. 2. Same-sex marriage--Juvenile literature. I. Scherer, Lauri S.
   HQ1034.U5G39 2014
   306.84'8--dc23
                                                                    2014000756

Printed in the United States of America
1 2 3 4 5 6 7 18 17 16 15 14

# Contents

## Chapter 3: What Effect Would Gay Marriage Have on Society?

# Foreword

Indulging in a wide spectrum of ideas, beliefs, and perspectives is a critical cornerstone of democracy. After all, it is often debates over differences of opinion, such as whether to legalize abortion, how to treat prisoners, or when to enact the death penalty, that shape our society and drive it forward. Such diversity of thought is frequently regarded as the hallmark of a healthy and civilized culture. As the Reverend Clifford Schutjer of the First Congregational Church in Mansfield, Ohio, declared in a 2001 sermon, "Surrounding oneself with only like-minded people, restricting what we listen to or read only to what we find agreeable is irresponsible. Refusing to entertain doubts once we make up our minds is a subtle but deadly form of arrogance." With this advice in mind, Introducing Issues with Opposing Viewpoints books aim to open readers' minds to the critically divergent views that comprise our world's most important debates.

Introducing Issues with Opposing Viewpoints simplifies for students the enormous and often overwhelming mass of material now available via print and electronic media. Collected in every volume is an array of opinions that captures the essence of a particular controversy or topic. Introducing Issues with Opposing Viewpoints books embody the spirit of nineteenth-century journalist Charles A. Dana's axiom: "Fight for your opinions, but do not believe that they contain the whole truth, or the only truth." Absorbing such contrasting opinions teaches students to analyze the strength of an argument and compare it to its opposition. From this process readers can inform and strengthen their own opinions, or be exposed to new information that will change their minds. Introducing Issues with Opposing Viewpoints is a mosaic of different voices. The authors are statesmen, pundits, academics, journalists, corporations, and ordinary people who have felt compelled to share their experiences and ideas in a public forum. Their words have been collected from newspapers, journals, books, speeches, interviews, and the Internet, the fastest growing body of opinionated material in the world.

Introducing Issues with Opposing Viewpoints shares many of the well-known features of its critically acclaimed parent series, Opposing Viewpoints. The articles are presented in a pro/con format, allowing readers to absorb divergent perspectives side by side. Active reading questions preface each viewpoint, requiring the student to approach the material thoughtfully and carefully. Useful charts, graphs, and cartoons supplement each article. A thorough introduction provides readers with crucial background on an issue. An annotated bibliography points the reader toward articles, books, and websites that contain additional information on the topic. An appendix of organizations to contact contains a wide variety of charities, nonprofit organizations, political groups, and private enterprises that each hold a position on the issue at hand. Finally, a comprehensive index allows readers to locate content quickly and efficiently.

Introducing Issues with Opposing Viewpoints is also significantly different from Opposing Viewpoints. As the series title implies, its presentation will help introduce students to the concept of opposing viewpoints and learn to use this material to aid in critical writing and debate. The series' four-color, accessible format makes the books attractive and inviting to readers of all levels. In addition, each viewpoint has been carefully edited to maximize a reader's understanding of the content. Short but thorough viewpoints capture the essence of an argument. A substantial, thought-provoking essay question placed at the end of each viewpoint asks the student to further investigate the issues raised in the viewpoint, compare and contrast two authors' arguments, or consider how one might go about forming an opinion on the topic at hand. Each viewpoint contains sidebars that include at-a-glance information and handy statistics. A Facts About section located in the back of the book further supplies students with relevant facts and figures.

Following in the tradition of the Opposing Viewpoints series, Greenhaven Press continues to provide readers with invaluable exposure to the controversial issues that shape our world. As John Stuart Mill once wrote: "The only way in which a human being can make some approach to knowing the whole of a subject is by hearing what can be said about it by persons of every variety of opinion and studying all modes in which it can be looked at by every character of mind. No wise man ever acquired his wisdom in any mode but this." It is to this principle that Introducing Issues with Opposing Viewpoints books are dedicated.

# Introduction

For much of the early twenty-first century, the fight to legalize same-sex marriage focused on classic pro-con debates, including whether same-sex marriage threatens or complements traditional marriage, whether it positively or negatively affects children, and whether it qualifies as a right that should be extended to everyone regardless of sexual orientation. In the early days of these debates, many gay Americans felt compelled to support what was seen as a key civil right, and many straight Americans often assumed that the majority of gay couples would take advantage of the ability to get married if they were legally allowed to do so.

Yet as the notion of same-sex marriage becomes more accepted, and as the arguments for and against it evolve from simple pro-con positions to more in-depth explorations of what marriage is and is for, gay Americans have felt freer to express more nuanced opinions on the issue. In doing so, they have revealed that many same-sex couples lack interest in getting married, even as they support the right of their counterparts to do so. Indeed—like heterosexuals—simply because gay couples *can* legally marry does not mean they will, and in doing so they may even risk compromising what it means to be a member of the gay community.

It is increasingly argued by gay Americans that marriage threatens one of the factors that make the community special and valuable: its long-standing identity as a radical, alternative movement. Indeed, mainstreaming the gay community through marriage is antithetical to the ways in which it has for decades explored sexual, social, political, and cultural ideas and lifestyles that are significantly and importantly different from the general society. Columnist Megan McArdle is one of many who have argued that the legalization of same-sex marriage—while good for rights, equality, and broad acceptance of homosexuality—tames the gay community to the point where it threatens to become stripped of the freedom and experimentation that have historically defined it; qualities that have been proudly embraced by its members. "Once gays *can* marry, they'll be expected to marry. And to buy sensible, boring cars that are good for car seats," warns McArdle. "You thought the fifties were conformist? Wait until all those fabulous [gay] 'confirmed bachelors' and maiden schoolteachers are expected to ditch their cute little one-bedrooms and join the rest of America in whining about crab grass, HOA [home owners' association] restrictions, and the outrageous fees that schools want to charge for overnight soccer trips."[1] From this perspective, participating in the institution of marriage distances the gay community from many of the qualities that have made it culturally and socially exciting, unique, and important.

A Pew Research Center survey taken in June 2013 surprisingly revealed that fewer gay Americans would take advantage of marriage than might be expected, given the ferocity with which the battle to legalize same-sex marriage has been waged. The survey polled nearly twelve hundred gay respondents and found that regardless of their opinion on whether gay marriage should be legal, 27 percent of unmarried respondents said they were not sure they were interested in ever getting married; this was significantly more than the 13 percent of those in the general population who said this. Of the unmarried gay respondents, only about half—52 percent—said they were interested in marrying someday, while 15 percent said they definitely did not want to ever get married. "It's a very, very archaic model," explains Sean Fader, a gay artist who lives in New York City. "It's this oppressive Christian model that says 'Pick a person that's going to be everything to you, they have to be perfect, then get a house, and have kids, and then you'll be happy and whole.'"[2]

Research by sociologist Kathleen Hull of the University of Minnesota bears this out. Hull's research shows that while the lesbian, gay, bisexual, and transgender (LGBT) community strongly supports the right of same-sex couples to marry, many are less certain they want to personally take advantage of the institution should it become available to them. "Some gays and lesbians clearly want to get married, but others are unsure or reject marriage for themselves,"[3] says Hull. One reason is because gay couples are wary of whether marriage is a good fit for their relationships: Fifty percent of respondents in Hull's research said they were ambivalent about marriage because they do not necessarily regard it as a good relationship model. Only about one-third thought it was, while about one-fifth thought it was a bad model. As Dan Dinero, a gay PhD-candidate puts it, "The problem with gay marriage [is that] it forces queers to fit into a very straight-centered way of life."[4]

Other gay couples actively reject the institution of marriage because of its history of subjugating women. Indeed, many want no part of an institution that has for much of its history put men and women on unequal footing, relegated women to child rearing and domestic work inside the home and made them subservient to their husbands. Says lesbian Dawne Moon, who is in a stable relationship with her partner and with whom she has a child, "The institution of marriage has a really bad history in terms of feminist issues—women being exchanged as property."[5] Sociologist Mary Bernstein, coeditor of the book *The Marrying Kind? Debating Same-Sex Marriage Within the Lesbian and Gay Movement,* agrees. "Part of the history of marriage has often disadvantaged women," she says. "Part of it is the association of marriage with inequality toward women."[6]

Thus, for many gay and lesbian Americans, the prospect of legalized same-sex marriage represents a double-edged sword, a bargain they are unsure they want to accept. On the one hand, marriage would afford them multiple legal rights and long-sought social acceptance; on the other, it risks undermining the alternative nature of the gay community. As lesbian writer Natalie Neusch has observed, there is an "insidious anxiety lurking beneath the surface of our gay-marriage win. It's the unsettling possibility that we've spent the past couple of decades fighting to fit into an institution that doesn't necessarily fit us. . . . We've been so focused on getting marriage 'equality' that we've hardly stopped to think about how we'd feel about actually being married."[7]

Exploring such nuanced implications of legalized gay marriage is just one of the many topics touched on in *Introducing Issues with Opposing Viewpoints: Gay Marriage.* The wealth of information and perspectives provided in the article pairs will help students come to their own conclusions about same-sex marriage and whether it should be legal in the United States.

## Notes

1. Megan McArdle, "Why Gay Marriage Will Win, and Sexual Freedom Will Lose," Daily Beast, March 26, 2013. www.thedaily beast.com/articles/2013/03/26/why-gay-marriage-will-win-and -sexual-freedom-will-lose.html.

2. Quoted in Cara Buckley, "Gay Couples, Choosing to Say 'I Don't,'" *New York Times,* October 25, 2013. www.nytimes.com/2013/10/27/style/gay-couples-choosing-to-say-i-dont.html?emc=eta1&_r=0.

3. Quoted in Sharon Jayson, "Not All Gays and Lesbians Want to Marry, Research Shows," *USA Today,* June 29, 2013. www.usatoday.com/story/news/nation/2013/06/27/same-sex-marriage-research/2465023.

4. Quoted in Natalie Neusch, "Gays Who Don't Want Gay Marriage," Daily Beast, February 26, 2012. www.thedailybeast.com/articles/2011/02/26/gays-who-dont-want-gay-marriage.html.

5. Quoted in Jayson, "Not All Gays and Lesbians Want to Marry."

6. Quoted in Jayson, "Not All Gays and Lesbians Want to Marry."

7. Neusch, "Gays Who Don't Want Gay Marriage."

# Chapter 1

# Should Gay Marriage Be Legal?

The issue of gay marriage has moved to the forefront of political debate in the United States.

# Same-Sex Marriage Is a Constitutional Right, Not a Democratic Issue

*"The case for marriage equality for same-sex couples should be obvious."*

**Dahlia Lithwick and Sonja West**

In the following viewpoint Dahlia Lithwick and Sonja West argue that marriage is a right that should be afforded to same-sex couples. They explain that previous Supreme Court cases have established marriage as a fundamental freedom, a basic right that cannot be denied to law-abiding Americans. Prohibiting same-sex marriage, therefore, violates the rights such people are due under the Constitution. Furthermore, Lithwick and West argue that same-sex marriage must not be decided state by state but at the national level, as people's rights must not be dependent on the zip code in which they live. The authors conclude that same-sex marriage must be legalized across the United States if the rights, liberties, and dignity of homosexual Americans are to be protected, as is called for under the Constitution.

Lithwick covers the courts and law for *Slate*, an online magazine, and West is an associate professor at the University of Georgia School of Law.

## AS YOU READ, CONSIDER THE FOLLOWING QUESTIONS:
1. What did the Supreme Court decide in the 1967 case *Loving v. Virginia,* as reported by the authors?
2. What does the Fourteenth Amendment offer the case for legalizing same-sex marriage, according to the authors?
3. What, according to Lithwick and West, do homosexual persons have in common with racial minorities and women?

When President Obama announced his support of same-sex marriage, he talked broadly about "equality" and "fairness." He spoke of "opposing discrimination against gays and lesbians" and making sure that nobody is treated as "less than full citizens when it comes to their legal rights." It was a powerful moment—historic and emotional. In the Aaron Sorkin version, the orchestra would have soared at this point as the supporting cast members exchanged teary-eyed yet knowing nods.

But then President Obama described how these rights should be protected and the music stopped with a squawk. Same-sex marriage, he said, is not in fact a federal issue but should be left to the states. He praised as "a healthy process and a healthy debate" the current patchwork of state referenda, amendments, laws, and judicial opinions that our marriage federalism has produced. He said he didn't want "to nationalize this issue" and added that the states are "working through this issue . . . all across the country." Adam Serwer and the *New York Times* editorial page were quick to point out that this doesn't represent much equality and fairness for Americans who live in, say, North Carolina, a state that just did away with both gay marriage and civil unions by referendum. Lyle Denniston goes further, suggesting that the president opposes the Defense of Marriage Act because it's an attempt to federalize marriage.

The "marriage is a purely state issue" rhetoric has been around for some time. It's become a familiar default argument, maybe because it sounds fair and feels safe. But having "evolved" this far on gay marriage, the time has come to evolve our own thinking on what is really at stake when we talk about marriage equality. We must embrace that this is a constitutional and not a democratic issue. Equality is not a popularity contest. This is hardly a radical argument. It's Supreme Court doctrine: Our rights to be treated as equal and full citizens do not evaporate when we cross state lines. Rather there are certain essential liberties, even in the realm of marriage, we all enjoy regardless of our ZIP code.

Obama wasn't technically wrong to observe that states have broad latitude to fashion their own marriage rules and usually have to recognize marriages solemnized in other states. But that state power has important constitutional limitations. The Supreme Court recognized, in its landmark 1967 decision in *Loving v. Virginia* that the "right to marry is of fundamental importance for all individuals" and "one of the vital personal rights essential to the orderly pursuit of happiness." After *Loving,* marriage is deemed a "fundamental freedom" protected by the Constitution, and states cannot deny an individual this basic right without an exceedingly good reason. If it's not a good enough reason for a state to prohibit someone from getting married because he committed a crime or failed to pay child support, then it's clearly not enough that he happens to be gay.

We pause now for a quick constitutional law primer: The Supreme Court has decided marriage cases under both the Due Process and Equal Protection Clauses of the 14th Amendment. The Due Process Clause protects fundamental rights while the Equal Protection Clause prohibits discrimination. Seen as a denial of a fundamental right under the Due Process Clause, the case for marriage equality for same-sex couples should be obvious. Viewed as a matter of discrimination under the Equal Protection Clause it becomes slightly more complicated. The court has acknowledged that certain groups of people are more likely to face discrimination and thus it demands more of the government when it tries to treat them differently. The court has been coy, however, about telling us whether people who are denied a government benefit based on their sexual orientation receive this kind of heightened protection. But the logic for stronger constitutional protection is undeniable. Like racial minorities and women, homosexuals as a group have historically faced societal and government discrimination based on a personal characteristic they cannot control. Thus, as with race and gender, the federal courts must be the guardians of justice and ensure that they are treated equally. That is the argument Cory Booker, mayor of Newark, N.J. has been advancing most vocally.

But if we're right that this is such a clear federal constitutional issue, then why have both liberals and conservatives continued to insist that this is a matter best left to the states? Two reasons. The first reflects our country's unique way of dealing with social change through an initial debate at the state level. And the second acknowledges that up until now it made strategic sense.

## FAST FACT

A 2013 poll by CNN/ Opinion Research Corporation found that 56 percent of respondents expressed support for legalizing same-sex marriage.

Much as we may love the idea of our court as the fearless defender of our liberties, as a practical matter, the court has always worked in tandem with the public on matters of civil rights. From slavery to segregation to abortion, we as a nation begin our discussions at the local level. We debate, we argue, we vote, and we enact laws. In theory, the arc of justice is long but we all get there eventually. When the time is right, the court steps in to solidify the consensus, frame the constitutional role, and force acceptance by the outliers. That's what happened in the civil rights era.

If the court, however, acts too early or misjudges trends, it risks generating a public backlash, perceptions of illegitimacy, and, once, a civil war. Thus timing is everything. When it works smoothly, it looks like *Loving v. Virginia*, where the court ruled that state anti-miscegenation laws were unconstitutional. At the time, there were only 16 states that still outlawed interracial marriage. Clearly the tide had turned and it was time for the court to act. Less smooth, however, was *Brown v. Board of Education*. When Brown was

*Federal judge Vaughn Walker wrote in his decision overturning California's Proposition 8 ballot initiative that there is a right to marry the person you love.*

decided, the opposition to school desegregation was much stronger and there was no obvious consensus or trend. While universally revered now, it took a contentious and violent decade and every branch of the federal government to ultimately enforce that court decision.

Later in *Roe v. Wade*, there were signs that the states were already peacefully resolving the issue. Thirteen states had passed laws permitting abortion in the prior 10 years and a number of court decisions had ruled other prohibitions invalid or ineffective. The court's decision, however, ignited the abortion wars that have been a staple of our time. An enormous amount of constitutional research suggests that *Roe v. Wade* may have hurt the cause of reproductive freedom by forcing the issue onto the country before Americans were ready. (There is also persuasive research to suggest otherwise, but this has become something of a truism when talking about the court and social change.)

Thus the question is a tactical one, not a constitutional one: Is the timing right to move the debate from the state to the federal battlefield? Are we all ready for *Brown* or detonating *Roe*? With marriage equality there is no consensus position. Currently states span the spectrum from constitutional bans to full marriage rights with plenty of "civil unions" and "domestic partnerships" occupying the middle. There are arguments that the trend favors marriage equality (opinion polls and the bulk of the recent movement among states have been in favor of marriage equality), but you can't just ignore 30 states with same-sex marriage bans.

There are more important practical distinctions with *Brown* and *Roe*, however, than just approximating the head count of the state laws. And here it's important to distinguish arguments about states rights and civil rights. Part of the problem the court experienced with *Brown* and *Roe* was that they were messy. *Brown* was almost too messy to implement and *Roe* was pretty much too messy to write. In its original *Brown* decision, the court didn't even try to figure out how to desegregate the schools, which ultimately involved a complicated system of busing and regulation. The *Roe* case, meanwhile, required a difficult parsing of stages of pregnancy and hinged on a vague standard of viability that changed with advances in medicine. The court produced an opinion that looked too much like legislation and not a judicial decision. Both of these problems opened the court up to criticisms that it was activist, micro-managing, and anti-democratic.

That is not the case with marriage equality. A federal constitutional opinion would be easy to write and easy to implement. Judge Vaughn Walker already wrote it in his decision about the Prop 8 ballot initiative. There is a right to marry the person you love. Americans cannot be discriminated against simply because of their sexual preference. Justice Anthony Kennedy could go to town with the "poetry of the law." It wouldn't be messy; it would be beautiful.

You wanna know what is messy? What's messy is what we have now—an oddball collection of marriage laws, civil unions, and same-sex bans that stop and start at state lines. This is simply unworkable in a country where we all have the right to travel (another one of those "fundamental rights") and there's no way to ask people to check their marriages at the border. Add to the mix that nobody has any idea whether the Defense of Marriage Act can overrule the Full Faith and Credit Clause by telling states that don't recognize same-sex marriages that they can ignore unions from states that do. We have interstate child custody disputes that are Solomonic in scope. And our schizophrenic tax codes treat the same couple as married on one form and not married on the next. Social Security, Medicaid, health care directives, estate planning, and immigration all hinge on marital status, which in turn hinges on the whim of the voters. The courts are just now wading into that morass and we won't lie, it's ugly out there.

The current system is unsustainable. Just as our country couldn't go on with a mix of free states and slave states, we cannot continue with this jumble of equal marriage states and discriminatory states. Recognizing a federal constitutional right is the only, and the best, method to put this issue to rest.

Advocates (perhaps including the president) will say that the timing is wrong. Gay-rights supporters learned all too well with *Bowers v. Hardwick* that an ill-timed, unfavorable decision can set back their cause by decades. But eventually we do reach a tipping point where, as a country, we need to address this as the federal civil rights issue it truly is. Or more appropriately, we need to acknowledge that basic equality is not subject to popular vote, even when majorities would like it to be. President Obama's announcement, we believe, knocked our country over that tipping point, but it needs to go further. The court has been clear that we can go further.

It's time to fight this battle where it belongs, which is on the federal stage. It's time to embrace the language of constitutional justice. It's time to say what is at stake here—true equality, full citizenship for everyone, basic human dignity and, yes, a fundamental right. The state-by-state rhetoric gives too much credence to the argument that the states have an option to discriminate, sometimes, so long as enough of their citizens cast a vote. They don't. The Constitution forbids it.

## EVALUATING THE AUTHOR'S ARGUMENTS:

Dahlia Lithwick and Sonja West argue in this viewpoint that the government has an interest in legalizing gay marriage because of its interest in ensuring that vulnerable groups are treated equally and enjoy the rights guaranteed them by the Constitution. In the following viewpoint Monica Migliorino Miller argues that the government has a fundamental interest in opposing gay marriage because of its interest in ensuring the future of society, which is contingent upon the bearing of children. In your opinion, which is the government's primary interest—protecting vulnerable groups' rights or ensuring the future of society? Are these necessarily mutually exclusive in the case of same-sex marriage? Explain your reasoning.

**Viewpoint**

**2**

# Gay Marriage Should Not Be Legal

## Monica Migliorino Miller

*"Homosexual persons . . . simply do not have the right to marry."*

Gay marriage is not "real" marriage and should thus not be legally sanctioned, argues Monica Migliorino Miller in the following viewpoint. According to Miller, marriage is an institution that is above human choices—it is the social mechanism through which the human race is perpetuated and thus upon which the future of society is dependent. In the author's opinion, marriage revolves around the ability to procreate children, which same-sex couples are unable to do. Because having children contributes to the stabilization and perpetuation of society, Miller argues that the state has an interest in protecting it. Therefore, in her opinion, the government cannot legalize same-sex marriage because of its need to protect marriage for the sake of social continuity. Miller concludes that heterosexuals must do a better job of defending the sacred institution that is at the heart of society.

Miller is a theology professor at St. Mary's College of Madonna University in Orchard Lake, Michigan.

**AS YOU READ, CONSIDER THE FOLLOWING QUESTIONS:**
1. Why, according to Miller, is homosexual activity not equivalent to heterosexual activity?
2. What does the phrase *blood-ties* mean as used by the author?
3. How have heterosexuals contributed to the dissolution of marriage, according to Miller?

L egal recognition of homosexual bonds as marital bonds ultimately means that gender, human sexuality, being a husband or a wife, motherhood and fatherhood have no objective moral meaning. This also means that the family itself has no objective moral meaning. The moral law rooted in nature is completely dissolved. There would no longer be any natural familial moral bonds, thus no longer any natural moral ties and thus no innate moral responsibilities arising from the very nature of the family.

## Marriage Is Not Merely Volitional

If the bond between two men or two women may be considered the equivalent of the one-flesh marital unity between a man and a woman, a bond that gives rise to children and the family, we are then saying that all human ties are strictly a matter of the will—only when *persons choose* to be connected to one another—by emotional, legal or artificial contrivance—are they then connected. And if the fundamental building block of society, namely the family, is essentially a matter of choice, those choices can be *undone* by mere personal volition. The family simply becomes a fragile arrangement of the will—no one is in *essence* a mother, a father, a husband or wife. The family unit is turned into a mere fragile arrangement of personal volition. Indeed, being a husband or wife, mother or father is nominal, not real.

The family is no longer a unit cemented by innate natural familial bonds that actually cause persons to *be* mother and child, brother and sister—essential identities imbedded in nature itself that produce inherent responsibilities to which persons who have such identities must be held accountable. Nothing here should be interpreted to mean that sterile couples who adopt children are not parents. Their heterosexual marital unity, unlike homosexual pairings, participates in the truth of marriage and is a public sign of that truth. A married couple who are incapable of procreating children by a pathology—nonetheless are still capable of honoring the life-giving *meaning* of their sexual intimacy. Their bond still contributes to the public support of the cultural, social and moral meaning of marriage. Their sexual unity is oriented towards life and the family in a way that gay sexual activity can never be.

## Gay Relationships Are Dead Ends

It is simply a lie that lesbian or homosexual acts are equivalent to sexual activity between a wedded man and woman. I will even go on and say that making them equivalent is an insult to the very meaning of marriage and the family. Gay sex is self-enclosed, of itself sterile and a societal dead-end. Since the family cannot come from such sex—the government does not have a compelling interest in protecting such unions.

FAST FACT

As of December 2013 gay marriage was explicitly banned in thirty-three states.

Why must the law protect marriage—and when I say "marriage" I mean, of course, the lifelong bond between a man and a woman upon which the family is built? Sex between a married man and woman is categorically different from gay sex. It is sex that confirms the meaning of masculinity and femininity—and it is sex that confers responsibilities that arise from the commitment of husbands and wives, especially when, from such sexual acts, new human beings are conceived. Society, *indeed the entire future of the world*, depends on these kinds of stable sexual unions that provide the necessary innate security for children. For this reason alone, the government has an interest in protecting marriage.

## Marriage Must Lead to Children

Indeed if someone needs a cogent argument as to why the government must make a distinction between homosexual bonds and marriage—here it is: When a man and woman commit themselves to a lifelong

*The author, Monica Migliorino Miller, right, organizes an abortion protest. Miller believes that marriage is an institution that is above human choices—it is the social mechanism through which the human race is perpetuated and thus upon which the future of society is dependent.*

unity of their persons—it is this type of union that leads to the begetting of children. The state has an interest in recognizing and protecting the unity between spouses and the natural blood relationships that are created by sexual marital activity. We need to take very seriously the importance of blood-ties in the building of society and culture. It is, indeed, these innate blood-ties that societies actually depend on for moral order and structure—beginning with the bond between a man and a woman that then creates the natural bonds of blood within the family itself. There is simply no substitution for this kind of cultural/societal building block. The state must support and protect marriage itself that creates the dynamic of the family unit, the unit that gives society its most sure, built-in, stable set of human identities and responsibilities.

Society is *not* the consequence of arbitrary self-willed human relationships. Of course engaged couples "choose" each other—but they do not choose the actual meaning of marriage. They do not "decide for themselves"—what it is they are about to enter. The meaning of marriage precedes them. As stated above, marriage, as it is related to the building of the family, not only produces identity and responsibilities within the "limited" nuclear family—it is the first building block that creates, not only brothers and sisters, but future marriages that produce cousins, nieces, nephews, uncles, aunts, grandfathers, grandmothers, great grand-fathers and mothers, as well as great uncles and aunts. Laws do not create these worlds—innate natural bonds—blood ties—create these worlds—worlds that of themselves cause human identity and human responsibili-ties. Absolutely nothing can replace such natural world-building! And the law cannot create the moral responsibilities that come from such bonds—it can only call persons to live up to them! Again, for this reason, government has an interest in protecting marriage.

## Heterosexual Couples Have Failed to Protect Marriage

How did we come to this point—that homosexual bonds should be considered the equivalent of marriage? The truth must be told. It is indeed the heterosexual community that is to blame, not homosexu-als. Heterosexuals have given up on the meaning of human sexual-ity. Heterosexuals are the ones who no longer believe in marriage. We have said so with 50 years of contraception, unquestioned sexual activity outside of marriage, living together without marriage, ram-pant divorce, including no-fault divorce, epidemic out-of-wedlock pregnancy rates, artificial reproduction—and then add to this—40 years of abortion. Heterosexuals have already said that sex, marriage and the family have no meaning—these become what we subjectively, privately, by a sheer matter of the will, say they are—and nothing more. We simply have no moral, cultural place to stand upon which we may say that homosexuals can't call what they do "marriage." After all, most heterosexual activity isn't marriage either! It too is dead-end sex that cannot carry the world into the future. . . .

## A Battle Based on Truth, Not Hate

Those who defend marriage as an institution between one man and one woman face fierce opposition. Gay rights activists, and their allies in the media, accuse defenders of marriage of being motivated from hate—a hate based on a narrow-minded intolerance, sheer bigotry, and an out-dated religious point of view. This depiction is intended to discredit and demoralize those who are opposed to "gay marriage" and circumvent any possible debate on the subject. Gay rights activ-ists argue that to deny persons with same-sex attraction the right to marry is to deny them the personal happiness and sense of dignity that heterosexuals enjoy—and thus the fairness card is played as a way to elevate such partnerships to the level of marriage.

Defense of marriage has nothing to do with hate. Rather this entire controversy has to do with the nature of objective reality itself. It has to do with the essence of what it means to be embodied persons and the way in which such embodiment leads to the foundation of the family. Those who oppose "gay marriage" are simply unwilling to locate the foundation of marriage and the family in precarious human feelings and emotions—which is the primary value upon which gay unions are formed and legitimized. No one can deny that such feelings are real, that such love is real, that the need for human intimacy between homosexuals and lesbians is real. It is simply that such private need is not the moral, legal equivalent of the institution of marriage, parenthood and the family that government has a duty to protect.

We must recognize that we are in a war for the truth, and it is a moral battle. This is not a time to be afraid to speak the truth. But speak always the truth in love—recognizing that homosexual persons have God-given dignity and basic human rights—and those rights must never be denied. But they simply do not have the right to marry—they do not have the rights to the privileges of marriage. Those who publicly defend marriage are going to be misunderstood, called names, mocked, belittled and derided. Nonetheless, those who understand what is at stake cannot hold back—the truth must be defended and marriage fought for—as civilization itself depends upon this sacred institution.

## EVALUATING THE AUTHOR'S ARGUMENTS:

To make her argument, viewpoint author Monica Migliorino Miller argues that marriage is defined by the ability to beget children. However, she makes an exception for infertile heterosexual couples, saying their unions still qualify as marriages even though they cannot have children. What is her reasoning? Do you agree, or think that that exception should be applied to same-sex couples as well? Why or why not?

**Viewpoint**

**3**

# Nine Justices or Fifty States? Who Should Decide Gay Marriage?

## Mark Davis

*"The states should decide [the legality of gay marriage] for themselves."*

Mark Davis is the host of a Salem Communications radio talk show, which airs in Dallas, Texas. In the following viewpoint he argues that voters, not courts, should decide whether to legalize gay marriage in their state. Davis argues that the issue of gay marriage is not one of equality the way that civil and women's rights are. When blacks or women were denied the right to vote, he says, they needed the Supreme Court to affirm their right to participate equally in society across all states. But in Davis's opinion, gay marriage is not an issue of equality but one of lifestyle and preference that is subject to a person's moral and religious nature. Therefore, it is an issue that should be decided by popular vote in each state, rather than judicial decree. Davis concludes that states should be free to legalize gay marriage if their voters agree to do so but should not be forced to by the courts since there is no constitutional right that is violated by its prohibition.

**AS YOU READ, CONSIDER THE FOLLOWING QUESTIONS:**
1. Why, according to Davis, should the wishes of children who have same-sex parents be disregarded when considering whether to legalize same-sex marriage?
2. What percentage of voters does the author say turned out in California to vote to legalize gay marriage?
3. When, according to Davis, is it acceptable to treat men and women differently under the law?

I would like to think that Supreme Court justices are smarter than I am.

At one level, they surely are. Their years of devotion to the practice and analysis of law involves countless pages of book-learning I will never undertake. Their brains must fairly bulge with minutiae I cannot grasp.

But there is a difference between intelligence and wisdom. There are high school dropouts who have deep wells of astuteness about how to think, act and live in an enlightened way. And there are Ph.D.'s I would not let into my house.

In one stunning moment Tuesday from the Supreme Court bench, we saw a very smart man say something of such profound stupidity that it should shake our very faith in some of the people who wear our loftiest judicial robes.

Justice Anthony Kennedy, who apparently has the power to shape a nation depending on which side of the bed he gets up on each day, was quizzing Charles Cooper on his defense of California's Proposition 8, which reflects the voters' wish for unique legal recognition of opposite-sex marriage.

"There are some 40,000 children in California . . . that live with same-sex parents, and they want their parents to have full recognition and full status. The voice of those children is important in this case, don't you think?"

Actually, Mister Justice Kennedy, that supposition has no place whatsoever in a consideration of what the Constitution says and what

*The author takes issue with Supreme Court justice Anthony Kennedy's (pictured) recent assertion that gay marriage should be allowed in California because the voices of the forty thousand children in that state who have same-sex parents should be heard.*

it does not. For a randomly-chosen person on the street not to know this is understandable—and the way things seem to be going lately, probable.

For a sitting Supreme Court Justice to invoke such a thing is shocking.

If we are going to start projecting the wishes of children onto our evaluations of various laws, divorce will become illegal immediately. And I would presume that there are over a million unborn babies who would prefer not to be ripped from the womb each year. I presume Justice Kennedy's ears are not cocked as attentively in their direction.

It is up to grownups to interpret law based on what the Constitution requires. That is a complex enough task without wringing our hands over emotional side-shows.

There are places for arguing our likes and dislikes of gay marriage—the states, where in the California example, a whopping voter turnout nearing 80 percent yielded a 52–48 victory for those seeking to legally recognize only the marriages between men and women. In that state, for the time being, that settles it.

As time passes, other states may join the ranks of those granting legal equivalency to homosexual unions. They are constitutionally permitted to do so. And that's where all of these battles should be.

Amid all the finger-wagging warning conservatives that they are on "the wrong side of history," we should be quick to remind that advocating liberty never offends history.

If a state wishes to engage in the radical redefinition of the central relationship in human history, it may do so. But proponents who win in one state do not have the right to dictate what happens elsewhere.

I am hopeful that the Supreme Court will leave this to the states, not because most justices share my state's rights passion, but because they ultimately do not want to wear a *Roe v. Wade*–style stain, cementing the reputation of another court relying not on the law but on the nebulous concept of The Way They Think Things Ought To Be.

Even liberals, who tend to favor "marriage equality," have a responsibility to respect the will of those who disagree.

> # FAST FACT
>
> Only one-third of respondents in a 2013 *New York Times*/CBS News poll felt that the legality of same-sex marriage should be decided by the federal government. Six in ten said it should be left to the states.

Something does not become a constitutional right simply when people grow passionate about it. I happen to think every restaurant should be able to allow smoking if it wishes, and every New York street vendor ought to be able to sell a barrel-sized Coke.

But cities may indeed constrain those matters with standards that are the will of the voters. (Remember that the Bloomberg soda ban did not fail constitutionally, it was nuked for incoherency).

There is no doubt that gay marriage proponents have successfully identified their cause as the moral cousin of the battles to end slavery and grant women's suffrage.

But civil rights and women's rights address areas where gender and race differences are irrelevant or none of the public's business. The sex of a voter or the race of a bus passenger are of no relative consequence, so equality under law is called for.

Men and women have equal status in many ways, but they are not the same type of human being. We have males and females because that dichotomy is central to the furtherance of the species. Throughout human history, men and women have interacted in ways that speak to the very different properties, characteristics and attributes they bring to the human table. Those differences are what make men and women unique, distinct and magnificent in their own ways.

The "marriage equality" movement that says it exists only to allow loving couples to do what they wish to do, brings the risk of eroding various gender differences, poisoning many other areas of law. If it is the same for me to marry a man as to marry a woman, how can we maintain any law that protects women uniquely, or restricts the draft to men, or keeps men out of ladies' rooms? Some examples run to the potentially absurd, but I would suggest our nation's founders find it mightily absurd that the nation they created is actually debating whether the nation should compel acceptance of a revision of one of life's fundamental precepts.

While there are factions ready to condemn any Republican failing to sing the glories of same-sex marriage, I believe there remain plenty of voters willing to accept national candidates who say the states should decide this matter for themselves.

The Bible guides our morality. It is properly used to bolster an argument against "marriage equality" in any state considering it. There

# Americans Think States Should Decide

A poll taken jointly by the *New York Times* and CBS News found that although most Americans approve of legalized same-sex marriage, the majority feel it is an issue that each state should decide for itself.

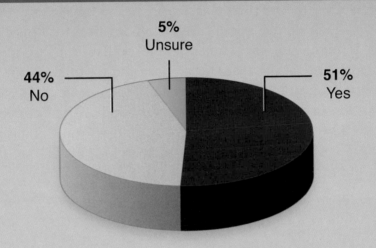

5%
Unsure

44%
No

51%
Yes

**Do you think laws regarding whether same-sex marriage is legal should be determined by the federal government or left for the states to decide?**

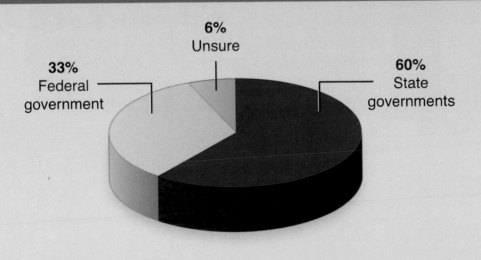

6%
Unsure

33%
Federal government

60%
State governments

Taken from: *New York Times*/CBS News, May 31–June 4, 2013.

are societal and historical reasons alongside that make this a wholly different thing than opposition to interracial marriage, which was an incursion into people's private business.

The Constitution guides our laws, which provide a legislative marketplace for those on both sides of the gay marriage issue.

Gays may marry any time anywhere and live as wedded couples for the rest of their lives in any state. The only issue is whether those unions will be viewed as the legal equal of heterosexual unions.

States wishing to take that giant step are free to legislate accordingly. Those unwilling may maintain unique recognition for opposite-sex couples. In both cases, the winners and losers have the responsibility to recognize that this is what liberty looks and feels like.

A judicial cram-down usurping voter wishes on this matter looks and feels like something wholly different. I hope Justice Kennedy and at least four of his colleagues can achieve clarity on this, fighting off the temptation to rule according to what seems kind to one side or popular in the polls.

## EVALUATING THE AUTHOR'S ARGUMENTS:

Viewpoint author Mark Davis and Elizabeth B. Wydra (author of the following viewpoint) disagree with each other over whether voters or judges should decide the legality of same-sex marriage. In your opinion, which author makes the better argument? Why? List at least two pieces of evidence (quotes, statistics, facts, or statements of reasoning) that caused you to side with one author over the other.

**Viewpoint**

**4**

# Courts Should Decide Whether Gay Marriage Should Be Legal

## Elizabeth B. Wydra

*"'Letting the states decide' [on gay marriage] is not what the Constitution demands."*

In the following viewpoint Elizabeth B. Wydra argues that courts must rule that gay marriage is legal because the right to marry is too important an issue to be put to popular vote in the states. Wydra contends that issues that involve key constitutional rights—such as marriage equality—are never left to popular vote; if that were the case, citizens of some states could vote to legalize slavery or to deny the right to vote to certain groups of people. Equality must never be subject to popularity, says Wydra; it is enshrined in the Constitution and must therefore be enforced via the courts. Furthermore, letting states decide gay marriage leads to a patchwork of inconsistent laws in which people's rights are upheld in certain regions and violated in others. Wydra concludes that only courts have the authority to enforce rights that are granted by the Constitution, which includes the right of same-sex couples to marry.

Wydra is chief counsel of the Constitutional Accountability Center, a law firm and public policy center.

**AS YOU READ, CONSIDER THE FOLLOWING QUESTIONS:**
1. What was at issue in the case *Hollingsworth v. Perry*, according to Wydra?
2. What two freedoms are so important that they are never put to a popular vote, according to the author?
3. How many states does Wydra say had laws against interracial marriage in 1967?

The Supreme Court Wednesday [June 26, 2013,] struck down Section 3 of the federal Defense of Marriage Act [DOMA]— which denied federal benefits to married gays and lesbians—as discriminatory and a violation of equal protection.

The court, however, declined to address the question raised by another important case, *Hollingsworth v. Perry*, about whether the right to marriage extended to gays and lesbians nationwide.

So, are supporters of marriage equality better off without the Supreme Court declaring that gay and lesbian couples have a constitutional right to marry?

## Certain Rights Are Too Important to Be Left to a Vote

Most Americans now back same-sex marriage, according to a recent poll, with younger voters the strongest supporters. A majority also believes, however, that the decision to recognize same-sex unions should be left up to individual states. As more states pass laws recognizing same-sex unions, some marriage equality supporters argue that advocates "shouldn't mess with progress." Or they worry about a backlash if the court were to recognize a right to marriage equality that would apply in all 50 states.

Regardless of whether it is sound political strategy to "take it slow," the fact is "letting the states decide" is not what the Constitution demands.

The Constitution enshrines certain rights and liberties as so important that they are above the politics of the day. Freedom of speech and religion, for example, are never put to a popular vote.

Though our federal system embraces state policy experimentation and diversity in many contexts, the Constitution was amended after the Civil War to take away from the states the ability to "experiment" with laws that perpetuate inequality. The Constitution does not allow a state to vote on reinstating segregation. Nor does the Constitution permit states to place a badge of inferiority on gay and lesbian couples and their families.

## Equality Must Be Granted, Not Voted On

The Supreme Court may be reluctant to unequivocally decide what it considers to be a hot-button social issue that is still percolating through the states. The Constitution, however, stands for the proposition that some rights cannot be left to the whims of a democratic majority. Equality before the law is one of those rights.

Consider our nation's history of racially discriminatory marriage laws. In 1967, while much of the nation had moved on from abhorrent antebellum attitudes about marriage between people of different races, 16 states still had laws on the books that prohibited interracial couples from marrying. Fourteen other states had repealed similar laws over the previous 15 years.

**FAST FACT**

One of many cases in which a court has overridden a state's constitution was *Romer v. Evans* in 1996. The US Supreme Court struck down Colorado's attempt to amend its constitution to implicitly allow discrimination based on sexual orientation.

But the Supreme Court did not decide to wait and see if the rest of the United States would follow suit when Mildred and Richard Loving, a black woman and a white man, asked the court to strike down Virginia's ban on interracial marriage.

Instead, the Supreme Court, in *Loving v. Virginia*, applied the Constitution's guarantees of equality and liberty to strike down Virginia's discriminatory marriage law as unconstitutional—striking down the other 15 state laws along with it.

The court's 1967 opinion noted that marriage is something traditionally left to the states. It observed that there was a long history

# Gay Rights and the Supreme Court

The Supreme Court has ruled on several major gay rights cases, most recently involving the issue of same-sex marriage.

## Bowers v. Hardwick—1986

The first major gay rights case to reach the Supreme Court. The Court ruled that a Georgia statute that criminalized sodomy was constitutional.

## Romer v. Evans—1996

The first Supreme Court victory on behalf of gays and lesbians enabled cities and counties to pass sexual orientation nondiscrimination ordinances.

## Lawrence v. Texas—2003

The Supreme Court overturned a Texas statute that criminalized sodomy, invalidating antisodomy laws across the country and for the first time making "gay sex" legal nationwide.

## United States v. Windsor—2013

The Supreme Court ruled it was unconstitutional for the Defense of Marriage Act (DOMA) to deny federal benefits to same-sex couples.

## Hollingsworth v. Perry—2013

The Supreme Court ruled that a California ballot initiative that prohibited same-sex marriage was invalid.

Taken from: National Gay and Lesbian Task Force, July 30, 2013. http://thetaskforceblog.org/2013/07/30/the-pathway-to-victory-a-review-of-supreme-court-lgbt-cases/.

of limiting marriage to persons of the same race—Virginia's law had roots in the colonial period. It acknowledged that the drafters of the 14th Amendment may not have originally intended the amendment to strike down laws prohibiting two people of different races from marrying. It also noted that some states had recently established more equitable marriage laws of their own accord.

Yet the Supreme Court still struck down Virginia's discriminatory marriage law—ruling it unconstitutional.

The Supreme Court should have followed this precedent in the challenge to California's ban on same-sex marriage.

## The Constitution Must Be Enforced

Yes, marriage is still a subject traditionally left to state regulation—but our Constitution places limits on how states can regulate marriage. Yes, our country has a long history of discriminating against gay and lesbian couples—but the court has repeatedly emphasized that the historical persistence of discrimination cannot save such practices from being struck down as unconstitutional.

After all, if a history of discrimination could carve out an exemption from the Constitution's guarantee of equality, we'd still have segregated schools.

In addition, the drafters of the 14th Amendment may not have been specifically thinking of gay and lesbian couples when they spoke of the need to ensure that the basic civil right of marriage was equally available to all. But the amendment's guarantee of "equal protection of the laws" is sweeping and universal. It protects all people, whether African-American or white, gay, lesbian or heterosexual, native-born or immigrant.

As the framers of the 14th Amendment recognized, the right to marry the person of one's choosing is a protected civil right, inherent in liberty and freedom; and the equality of rights secured by the amendment's Equal Protection Clause includes the equal right to marry the person of one's choice.

## Equality Should Not Be Subject to Popularity

By denying same-sex couples the right to marry, California's Proposition 8 contravenes this original meaning. Fortunately, today's ruling from the Supreme Court in the Prop 8 case leaves the federal district court's decision recognizing this fundamental right to stand. And Justice Anthony Kennedy's opinion in *Windsor*, striking down Section 3 of DOMA, has words of encouragement for gay and lesbian couples seeking recognition that their relationships are "worthy of dignity in the community, equal with all other marriages."

Given that the majority of Americans now support marriage equality, there is hope that other states will right this wrong on their own. But the Constitution tells us—in no uncertain terms—that this equality is not apportioned based on popularity or political convenience.

The Supreme Court should not shy away from applying the Constitution. Or its promise of equality for all could begin to ring hollow.

## EVALUATING THE AUTHOR'S ARGUMENTS:

In this viewpoint Elizabeth B. Wydra argues that states should never be allowed to put rights-related issues to a vote; people's rights should never be subject to popularity or public whim, lest states vote to have segregated schools or prevent women from voting. How do you think Mark Davis, the author of the previous viewpoint, would respond to this argument? Why? Quote from the texts in your answer.

**Viewpoint**

**5**

# Legalized Same-Sex Marriage Is Inevitable

## Michael J. Klarman

*"The ultimate outcome of the contest over gay marriage no longer seems in doubt."*

In the following viewpoint Michael J. Klarman argues that it is only a matter of time before same-sex marriage is legal in the United States. He says two main factors make gay marriage's legality inevitable. First, increasing numbers of Americans count gay people among their friends, family members, and coworkers, which has drawn more people to the cause of legalized gay marriage. With gay people more visible in society, the issues affecting their lives seem more personal and acceptable to those around them. Second, polls indicate increasing support for the right of gay couples to marry, especially among young people, whom Klarman predicts will carry this issue into the future. Klarman argues that conservatives' rampant opposition to gay marriage is another indication its legalization is at hand. He predicts gay marriage will eventually become legal but anticipates heated social, legal, and political battles along the way.

Klarman is a professor at Harvard Law School and the author of the book *Same-Sex Marriage Litigation and Political Backlash.*

**AS YOU READ, CONSIDER THE FOLLOWING QUESTIONS:**
1. What percentage of Americans does Klarman say know someone who is gay?
2. What percentage of Americans aged eighteen to thirty-four support gay marriage, as reported by Klarman?
3. Who is Albert Mohler and how does he factor into the author's argument?

The year 2012 is shaping up as a big one for same-sex marriage. Last week [in February 2012], the Washington state Legislature passed a bill allowing gay marriage, and legislatures in Maryland and New Jersey may follow suit shortly (though New Jersey Gov. Chris Christie has promised a veto). North Carolina and Minnesota are conducting referendums this year on constitutional amendments to bar gay marriage, and Maine is likely to conduct a referendum on legalizing it.

On Tuesday [February 7, 2012], the U.S. 9th Court of Appeals reminded us that courts too have something to say on the subject. In a case challenging the constitutionality of California's Proposition 8 [banning legal gay marriage], that court ruled in favor of gay marriage. Because its ruling was so narrow that it may not be applicable outside California, the U.S. Supreme Court may decide not to review this decision. Eventually, though, the Supreme Court will take a gay marriage case. How might the justices decide it when they do?

## The Supreme Court's Evolution on Gay Marriage

As recently as seven or eight years ago, there might not have been a single justice prepared to declare a federal constitutional right to same-sex marriage. Opinion polls then showed that Americans opposed gay marriage by a 2–1 margin, and a Massachusetts court decision declaring a right to gay marriage under the state constitution produced an enormous political backlash in 2004, with 13 states enacting constitutional bans. Even liberal justices such as Ruth Bader Ginsburg and Stephen G. Breyer, who probably sympathize with gay marriage, might well have been wary of venturing too far in advance of public opinion and stoking further political backlash.

The situation has since changed dramatically. Opinion polls now consistently show that a slender majority of Americans support gay marriage. State supreme courts in California, Connecticut and Iowa have ruled in its favor, and legislatures in five states have enacted gay-marriage statutes. If liberal judges on state supreme courts now regularly support gay marriage, liberal justices on the U.S. Supreme Court are likely to do so as well.

A number of constitutional issues today—abortion, affirmative action, campaign finance reform and the death penalty—divide the Supreme Court 5 to 4, with Justice Anthony Kennedy providing the critical swing vote. How might Kennedy approach the gay-marriage issue?

Kennedy often converts dominant social mores into constitutional commands to bring outlier states into line with the majority. In this case, the states that allow gay marriage are in a distinct minority, suggesting he might be reluctant to identify such a constitutional right.

*Polls indicate increasing support for the right of gay couples to marry, especially among young people, who the author predicts will carry this issue forward in the future.*

# Gay Marriage Is Here to Stay

A 2013 poll by the Pew Research Center found the majority of Americans say that legalization of same-sex marriage is "inevitable." Even those who oppose legalization believe it nonetheless will happen.

| | 2004 | 2013 |
|---|---|---|
| Percent who say legal recognition of same-sex marriage is inevitable | 59% | 72% |
| Among those who . . . | | |
|    Favor allowing gays to marry legally | 85% | |
|    Oppose allowing gays to marry legally | 59% | |

Taken from: Pew Research Center, May 1–5, 2013.

On the other hand, Kennedy has written the court's only two decisions supporting gay rights, and he comes from a part of the country—Northern California—where support for gay marriage is strong. Moreover, Kennedy seems especially attuned to his historical legacy, and if gay marriage is inevitable, then a court ruling in its favor will probably be seen one day as the *Brown vs. Board of Education* [the 1954 ruling desegrating schools and initiating society-wide desegregation] of the gay rights movement.

## Society Is More Gay Friendly than in the Past

Why is gay marriage inevitable? First, the basic insight of the gay rights movement over the last four decades has proved powerfully correct: As more gays and lesbians have come out of the closet, the social environment has become more gay friendly. In turn, as the social environment has become more hospitable, more gays and lesbians have felt free to come out of the closet. This social dynamic is powerfully reinforcing and unlikely to be reversed.

One factor that most strongly predicts support for gay equality is knowing someone who is gay. As more gays and lesbians come out of the closet, more parents, children, siblings, friends, neighbors and co-workers know or love someone who is gay. Because few people favor discrimination against those they know and love, every gay person coming out of the closet creates more supporters of gay equality.

The number of Americans reporting that they know somebody who is openly gay tripled between 1985 and 2000, reaching 75%. One study in 2004 found that among those who reported knowing someone who is gay, 65% favored either gay marriage or civil unions, while only 35% of those who reported not knowing any gay people supported them.

## Polls Show Increasing Support

A second reason that gay marriage seems inevitable is that young people so strongly support it. One study by political scientists found a gap of 44 percentage points between the oldest and youngest survey respondents in their attitudes toward gay marriage. A 2011 poll found that 70% of those age 18 to 34 supported gay marriage. It is hard to imagine a scenario in which young people's support for gay marriage dissipates as they grow older.

The trend in favor of gay marriage has accelerated dramatically in the last three years. Before 2009, the annual rate of increase in support for gay marriage was about 1.5 percentage points, but since then it has been closer to 4 percentage points. Statistical models predict that in another dozen years, every state will have a majority in favor of gay marriage.

**FAST FACT**

A May 2013 Pew Research Center poll found that 72 percent of Americans believe it is "inevitable" that the law will eventually recognize gay marriage.

## The War Seems Won but the Battle Is Not Over

In recent years, many conservatives have begun to acknowledge the inevitability of gay marriage, even as they continue to strongly oppose it. In March 2011, Albert Mohler, president of the Southern Baptist Theological Seminary, said on a Christian radio program that "it is clear that something like same-sex marriage . . . is going to become normalized, legalized and recognized in the culture."

"It's time," he continued, "for Christians to start thinking about how we're going to deal with that."

That a particular social change may be inevitable, given certain background conditions, does not mean that opponents will cease fighting it. White Southerners continued to massively resist *Brown* long after most of them came to believe that school desegregation was inevitable.

Similarly, those who believe that gay marriage contravenes God's will are not likely to stop fighting it simply because their prospects of success are diminishing. Moreover, because religious conservatives are both intensely opposed to gay marriage and highly mobilized politically, they are likely for the next several years to continue exerting significant influence over Republican politicians who need their support to win primary elections.

Although the ultimate outcome of the contest over gay marriage no longer seems in doubt, plenty of fighting remains until that battle is over.[1]

## EVALUATING THE AUTHOR'S ARGUMENTS:

In this viewpoint Michael J. Klarman suggests that increased visibility of gays in society along with higher support in the polls indicate that gay marriage is all but inevitable. How do you think each of the other authors in this chapter might respond to this suggestion? List each author and write two to three sentences on what you think his or her response might be and why.

1. In 2013 the Supreme Court heard two gay marriage cases—*United States v. Windsor* and *Hollingsworth v. Perry*. It ruled on the side of gay marriage in both of them, striking down a portion of the Defense of Marriage Act that denied federal benefits to same-sex partners in *Windsor* and rendering invalid a California ballot initiative that prohibited gay marriage in *Hollingsworth v. Perry*.

**Viewpoint**

**6**

# Legalized Same-Sex Marriage Is Not Inevitable

**Grant Dossetto**

*"The same sex marriage cause remains a loser in America."*

In the following viewpoint Grant Dossetto argues that legalized same-sex marriage is not necessarily inevitable. For one, same-sex marriage is much less popular than polls suggest: Although some have indicated that about half of all Americans support same-sex marriage, the overwhelming majority of people live in states that have voted to prohibit same-sex marriage. In Dossetto's opinion, this means that polls indicating fifty-fifty support of the issue are flawed. It also indicates that opposition to same-sex marriage occurs across a variety of races, ethnicities, income brackets, regions, political affiliations, and other markers. States that have prohibited same-sex marriage have not suffered economically or in population, which tells Dossetto that their lack of willingness to embrace gay marriage is not a big deal to many people. He concludes that same-sex marriage is not a winning cause or even one supported by impressive numbers of Americans.

Dossetto is a contributor to *American Thinker,* a conservative news-magazine.

**AS YOU READ, CONSIDER THE FOLLOWING QUESTIONS:**
1. What percentage of Americans at the time of this writing in May 2012 does Dossetto say lived in states in which same-sex marriage was illegal?
2. How many states does the author say had won constitutional ballot initiatives that prohibited same-sex marriage? How many states had won constitutional ballot initiatives that legalized same-sex marriage?
3. What, according to Dossetto, is the modern-day equivalent of the Fugitive Slave Act?

The passing of Amendment One in North Carolina, making the Tar Heel State the 32nd state in the country to enshrine in their constitution that marriage is between one man and one woman, created the predictable flurry of outrage among gay rights supporters. Shrill complaints of bigotry and homophobia with an added dose of backwardness filled up airwaves, Internet forums, and Facebook statuses all intended to smear the 88% of states and over 90% of Americans who now live where same sex-marriage is illegal as the worst kind of bigot and homophobe. Many in the gay rights community cloak their cause in grandiose terms. It is not simply another front in the culture war, a values vote issue. To supporters, gay rights have taken on more importance. If a state will not allow two members of the same sex to marry, then it is committing a violation of those people's inalienable human rights. These supporters' actions indicate something entirely different. In fact, there is a good case to be made that if you view same-sex marriage as a human rights violation, the worst offender is the same-sex-marriage supporter himself.

## Same-Sex Marriage Is Much Less Popular than Polls Suggest

National polling outlets such as Pew and Gallup put support for same-sex marriage at around 50%. If the country were truly nationally split, then it would seem impossible for traditional marriage to have the support that it has enjoyed in this century. Traditional marriage is now 32 for 32 on state constitutional ballots, enacted in centrist or outright liberal states, such as Maine and California in direct response to legislative statutes recognizing same-sex marriage, as well as plenty of traditional Democratic strongholds such as Minnesota and Michigan by overwhelming majorities. It passed in North Carolina, while garnering national attention, with over 60% of the vote. Traditional marriage support is truly a bipartisan platform which attracts people across race and income as well as political affiliation. Can this majority coalition truly be at its core nasty and bigoted? Conceding that point actually makes same-sex marriage supporters look worse.

There are many theories why same-sex marriage polls better than it performs at the ballot box. Some, such as Public Policy Polling tweeted on Tuesday, suggest a Bradley effect[1] on the issue—i.e., that the average voter will say to a pollster that he supports same-sex marriage to avoid being viewed as a bigot but vote differently at the polls. Another explanation appears more plausible, though, and that is that same-sex marriage is particularly popular among voting blocs who do not turn out to the polls in high numbers. Voting is not a difficult task, though, and even cynicism or disbelief in the political structure in your local capital or Washington, D.C., the usual excuse for not voting, rings awfully hollow when you have a chance to right a great—many say *the* great—moral wrong of our age. How can one claim that an issue is a human right and then refuse to make any sacrifice to vote on the issue? Gay rights, according to its supporters, are more than a school board election or art museum millage [tax]. It is modern slavery, modern Jim Crow [segregation], and the response to that is indifference and apathy? That is bigotry.

## Lukewarm Support Is Mistaken for Emphatic Endorsement

A failure to vote is not the only anti-gay behavior that occurs among the same-sex marriage crowd. Whom the same-sex marriage supporter votes for also exposes a terrible homophobia. This week [in May 2012]

---

1. The Bradley effect takes its name from popular former Los Angeles mayor Tom Bradley, who was black and far ahead in the polls in the 1982 California governor's race, yet lost the mayoral election to a white opponent; some social scientists explain the phenomenon as due to the fact that polled persons do not want to appear racist so they say they support the minority candidate yet in the secrecy of the voting booth vote for a white candidate.

*The author asserts that support for gay marriage is not as great as polls lead people to believe.*

[President] Barack Obama came out for same-sex marriage. His support was in no way unconditional, though; he carefully parsed that he personally supports the practice but that states have the right to decide. How many other issues has Obama determined were purely states' rights issues? Not health care, or border enforcement, or abortion, or even coal plant emissions, to name but a few issues that should fall below an innate human right. As Bruce Carroll, the creator of gaypatriot.org, wrote this week, replacing same-sex marriage with slavery in Obama's quotation sounds like something President James Buchanan would've said circa 1860:

> At a certain point, I've just concluded that—for me personally, it is important for me to go ahead and affirm that—I support abolishing slavery. Now—I have to tell you that part of my hesitation on this has also been I didn't want to nationalize the issue. There's a tendency when I weigh in to think suddenly it becomes political and it becomes polarized.

And what you're seeing is, I think, states working through this issue—in fits and starts, all across the country. Different communities are arriving at different conclusions, at different times. And I think that's a healthy process and a healthy debate. And I continue to believe that this is an issue that is gonna be worked out at the local level, because historically, this has not been a federal issue, what's recognized as abolishing slavery.

Buchanan is widely regarded as the worst president in the history of the Union. Why does Obama get a pass from the gay rights equal human rights crowd?

## Democrats Are Not Really Pro–Gay Rights

In fact, Barack Obama is three years behind [former Republican vice president] Dick Cheney in holding that position, yet there was no glee among the most ardent same-sex marriage supporters when the Republican said the same. Ted Olson, [George W.] Bush's solicitor general, is actively representing the gay rights movement in a case going to the Supreme Court, but the two Republicans' positions and active contributions to the cause are ignored because of their political affiliation. Obama in 1996 in Chicago said he supported gay marriage when it remained a fringe issue. He then publically switched opinions to supporting traditional marriage before halfway reversing this past week. There is no evidence that his private opinion ever wavered, but for at least the last eight years he was publicly dishonest in supporting same-sex marriage. To support Obama for president this year [2012] can show only that you are unserious about same-sex marriage politically. That would make you a bigot, using liberal standards on the issue. And yet, there is no doubt that pro-same-sex marriage advocates will do just that.

> **FAST FACT**
>
> Even in California, one of the states most supportive of gay rights, voters in 2008 passed Proposition 8, which defined marriage as being only "between a man and a woman."

The Democratic Party will receive the overwhelming majority of votes among same-sex marriage supporters who define the issue as a

As of late March 2014 only seventeen states, plus the District of Columbia, allow same-sex marriage, while thirty-three states have limitations on it. Some argue this indicates same-sex marriage is far from decided.

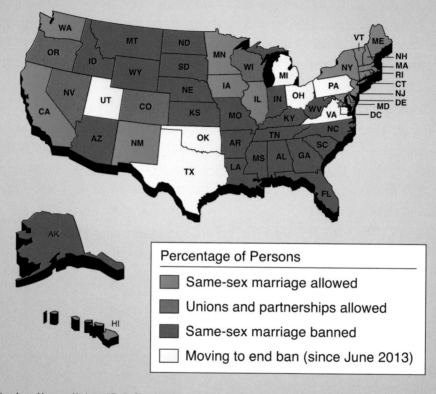

Taken from: Masuma Ahuja and Emily Chow. "Same-Sex Marriage Status in the U.S." *Washington Post*, March 23, 2014.

civil or human right, yet for two years it possessed filibuster-proof majorities in Congress and the executive branch and did nothing on same-sex marriage at the federal level. Is that not rank bigotry? Obama has modified his position only after he lost the votes to accomplish such a goal. He can now take one position comfortably, knowing that he will never have to sign into law a bill that holds him to it. We could not say that in 2009 or 2010, when he conveniently remained silent. The past twelve years of Democratic presidencies have produced only one piece of legislation in regard to same-sex marriage; the Defense of Marriage Act (DOMA). That legislation says that states that do not approve of same-sex marriage do not have to recognize marriages that occur in states which do. Imagine if you replace same-sex marriage with slavery, which is the far-left position on the issue. A Democratic president, Bill Clinton, signed into law the modern equivalent of the Fugitive Slave Act [that is, DOMA]. This was never overturned by Barack Obama, and gay rights opponents have treated the legislation far less hostilely than the North reacted to the idea that they were forced to recognize that certain blacks were due fewer human rights because they hailed from slave states in the South.

## A Loser of a Cause

States which do not allow for gay marriage are thriving. Iowa, New York, and Massachusetts didn't see population growth during the last census period of more than 4.1%. Anti-same-sex marriage states such as Texas or Arizona saw growth of over 20%. North Carolina saw growth of over 18%. Texas, among others, has enjoyed better economic growth and job-creation than Massachusetts or New York. Never before in human history have states or countries that chronically abused human rights managed that. The Southern states, the Soviet Union, North Korea—all lagged their peers who respected basic human dignity. That suggests that same-sex marriage isn't a human right or a human dignity issue, but is instead a political issue, and maybe even a minor one at that.

There is no sign that daily behavior is affected at all, even of same-sex marriage proponents, by a decision of a majority of voters in a state to define marriage using a traditional definition. This varies markedly from those who have suffered true human rights abuses. The same-sex marriage crowd is now 0–32 in votes on their cause. It is obvious why they are frustrated at the results. However, to scream defamatory accusations of bigotry and homophobia, when your own actions don't stand up to scrutiny because you've lost a political argument, is wrong. It cheapens actual human rights abuses, what true abuses against liberty do to the human soul. That is a reprehensible thing to do and may be a good reason why the same sex marriage cause remains a loser in America.

## EVALUATING THE AUTHOR'S ARGUMENTS:

In this viewpoint Grant Dossetto argues that same-sex marriage is far from inevitable. What pieces of evidence does he provide to support this claim? List at least three pieces of evidence you find compelling. Does he convince you of his argument? Why or why not?

# Chapter 2

# What Effect Would Gay Marriage Have on Families?

*Gay marriage's effects on family life has been an issue among advocates as well as opponents.*

# Gay Marriage Weakens the Institution of Marriage

## Riley Balling

*"Same-sex marriage will only . . . make it harder to promote traditional marriage."*

Riley Balling is an attorney in Minnesota. In the following viewpoint he argues that gay marriage weakens the institution of marriage—even negatively affecting his own marriage. Balling explains that marriage is a social institution with one purpose: to produce children. In his view, children must be the prime focus of a marriage, and their development and what they offer society and humanity trumps the relationship between a husband and wife. In Balling's view, modern culture has changed the meaning of marriage to be a vehicle of self-fulfillment for the spouses; same-sex marriage has been enabled by this change and cements this change to the understanding of marriage caused by our historically recent cultural shift. From the author's perspective, changing the nature of marriage from social betterment to personal fulfillment has grave consequences for all persons. He concludes that the definition of marriage cannot be changed without its negatively affecting everyone.

**AS YOU READ, CONSIDER THE FOLLOWING QUESTIONS:**
1. What does Balling say humans are motivated to do?
2. What effect does Balling say single-parent families have on crime?
3. What does the word *tertiary* mean as used by the author?

In the marriage debate, people frequently argue that how one chooses to define marriage doesn't affect other people's definitions of marriage, and because my definition is as good as yours, it should also be promoted by society.

Many times it is stated: "What I choose to do in my marriage doesn't affect your marriage." However, same-sex marriage affects all of our marriages.

## People Naturally Try to Change Society to Advance Their Identity

First, to explain, private actions have public effects. All our actions, both private and public, define our identity. Being human, we are motivated to impart our identity to future generations. As we have seen, and understandably so, people in homosexual relationships are trying to change society to more readily embrace and promote their view of their identity. This is possible largely due to the disassociation between sexual relationships and procreation.

In contrast, there are many who have not disassociated sex and children, and for reasons both secular and religious have incorporated heterosexual relationships into their identity. These people have generally been trying to live up to the ideal that marriage was established millennia ago to promote

## FAST FACT

The New Family Structures Study by the University of Texas–Austin found that out of over two hundred young adults who had a gay parent, only two said their parent maintained a relationship with the same person throughout their childhood. This suggests that same-sex relationships are unstable and unlikely to last long term.

## The Decline of Marriage

In 1960, 72 percent of American adults were married. By 2008 that share had fallen to 52 percent. Divorce and separation were also on the rise. Some argue that with the institution of marriage already vulnerable, it is unwise to redefine marriage to include same-sex couples.

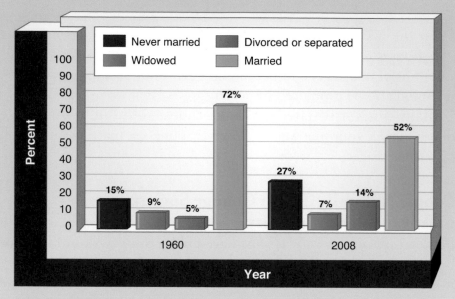

Note: Ages eighteen and older. Numbers may not total to 100 percent due to rounding.

Taken from: Pew Research Center, 2010.

the raising of children in safe environments supported by their biological parents.

Sadly, we don't always live up to this ideal, and most have experienced the trauma caused by a breaking family. However, we know of marriages that practically achieve the ideal, and we see the happiness that children find in a supportive family structure. Even though some traditional families are breaking, it doesn't mean the ideal of traditional marriage is broken.

Many studies show that single parents struggle to provide the safe environment provided by a two-biological-parent home. Bless the single parents who try, but there is a direct correlation between single homes and crimes of all types. If anything, the effects of broken homes indicate the importance of reestablishing the ideal of traditional marriage.

## The View of Marriage as a Means of Self-Fulfillment Endangers Children

Same-sex marriage falls short of producing safe environments for children because it, at the very least, reinforces changes to the marital definition. Historically, before the sexual revolution, society's definition of marriage was focused on the raising and bearing of children. A man married a woman; they had children, and did practically everything around the raising of those children. The interests of a parent became tertiary to the interests of their children and their spouse.

Currently, as a society, we have wavered from this traditional motivation, and many, not all, view marriage as a venue for self-fulfillment. This modern view is directly culpable for the rise in broken homes

*Opponents of gay marriage say that the main purpose of marriage is to produce legitimate children and that since gay couples cannot reproduce, calling gay unions marriage only weakens the institution.*

and its resulting negative effects. Because same-sex marriage is made possible by this modern view of marriage, if we make same-sex marriage equivalent to traditional marriage, we only more firmly impart to future generations that marriage is about personal fulfillment. The cementing of the modern view will only continue its destruction of safe environments for future generations.

## Changing the Definition of Marriage Changes the Influence a Society Exerts on Its Members

For many of us who favor traditional marriage, marriage is about raising children in a healthy environment. Thus, any change to the definition of marriage affects our marriage. Our "traditional" marriages and the children they produce are our greatest source of happiness, and we desire that our children will live in a world that will promote their ability to make the same choices that brought us happiness.

There are many who tout the modern definition, and we are susceptible to these influences. As we listen to these influences, we change our view of marriage and our marital relationship accordingly. Same-sex marriage will only increase these influences and make it harder to promote traditional marriage.

Although not all are able to participate in a traditional marriage that yields children, we all benefit by its establishment in creating strong homes for the next generation with strong direction from self-sacrificing parents. The disestablishment of this ideal affects us all.

## EVALUATING THE AUTHOR'S ARGUMENTS:

In this viewpoint Riley Balling uses examples and reasoning to make his argument that gay marriage threatens the institution of marriage. He does not, however, use any quotations to support his point. If you were to rewrite this article and insert quotations, what authorities might you quote from? Where would you place the quotations, and why?

# I Was Wrong About Same-Sex Marriage

*"Whatever is driving [the decline of traditional family and marriage], it seems more than implausible to connect it to same-sex marriage."*

**David Frum**

Gay marriage poses no threat to the institution of marriage, argues David Frum in the following viewpoint. Frum admits that for a long time he opposed gay marriage out of fear it would weaken the institution of marriage, hurt families, and threaten society's stability and morality. But these fears have not materialized as more same-sex couples have married in states that have legalized it, he contends. Although families and marriage continue to suffer from instability, they do so at a slower rate than prior to gay marriage's introduction and for reasons that have nothing to do with same-sex couples (such as the challenges of assimilating into a new country). Frum concludes that gay marriage poses no threat to the institution of marriage and could, if enough same-sex couples enter into loving, permanent relationships, even strengthen it.

Frum is a contributing editor at *Newsweek* and its website, the Daily Beast.

**AS YOU READ, CONSIDER THE FOLLOWING QUESTIONS:**
1. What event in New York State does Frum say made him realize he no longer opposes same-sex marriage?
2. What happened to marriage during the 1970s and 1980s, according to the author?
3. What does Frum observe about Hispanic families?

I was a strong opponent of same-sex marriage. Fourteen years ago, [journalist and gay-rights supporter] Andrew Sullivan and I forcefully debated the issue at length online (at a time when online debate was a brand new thing).

Yet I find myself strangely untroubled by New York state's vote to authorize same-sex marriage—a vote that probably signals that most of "blue" [Democratic Party–leaning] states will follow within the next 10 years.

I don't think I'm alone in my reaction either. Most conservatives have reacted with calm—if not outright approval—to New York's dramatic decision.

Why?

The short answer is that the case against same-sex marriage has been tested against reality. The case has not passed its test.

## Fears About Gay Marriage Were Wrong

Since 1997, same-sex marriage has evolved from talk to fact.

If people like me had been right, we should have seen the American family become radically more unstable over the subsequent decade and a half.

Instead—while American family stability has continued to deteriorate—it has deteriorated much more slowly than it did in the 1970s and 1980s before same-sex marriage was ever seriously thought of.

By the numbers, in fact, the 2000s were the least bad decade for American family stability since the fabled 1950s. And when you take a closer look at the American family, the facts have become even tougher for the anti-gay marriage position.

Middle-class families have become somewhat more stable than they used to be. For example: College-educated women who got married in the 1990s were much less likely to get divorced than equally educated women who got married in the 1970s.

## Family Problems Are Not Connected to Gay Marriage

What's new and different in the past 20 years is the collapse of the Hispanic immigrant family. First-generation Latino immigrants maintain traditional families: conservative values, low divorce rates, high fertility and—despite low incomes—mothers surprisingly often at home with the children.

But the second-generation Latino family looks very different. In the new country, old norms collapse. Nearly half of all children born to Hispanic mothers are now born out of wedlock.

Whatever is driving this negative trend, it seems more than implausible to connect it to same-sex marriage. How would it even work that a 15-year-old girl in Van Nuys, California, becomes more likely to have a baby because two men in Des Moines, Iowa, can marry?

Maybe somebody can believe the connection, but I cannot.

## Gay Marriage Is Not to Blame

I remain as worried as ever about the decline in family stability among poorer Americans. But as for same-sex marriage, my attitude follows the trajectory described nearly 150 years ago by the English writer Anthony Trollope in his novel "Phineas Finn."

Two of his characters are discussing a proposed reform that has just been defeated in Parliament. The author of the reform is understandably dejected. His friend consoles him by pointing to the future:

Many who before regarded legislation on the subject as chimerical [illusory], will now fancy that it is only dangerous, or perhaps not more than difficult. And so in time it will come to be looked on as among the things possible, then among the things probable;—and so at last it will be ranged in the list of those few measures which the country requires as being absolutely needed. That is the way in which public opinion is made.

By coincidence, I am writing these words on the morning of my own 23rd wedding anniversary. Of all the blessings life has to offer, none equals a happy marriage. If proportionally fewer Americans enjoy that blessing today than did 40 years ago, we're going to have to look for the explanation somewhere other than the Legislature in Albany [capital of New York].

## EVALUATING THE AUTHOR'S ARGUMENTS:

Viewpoint author David Frum admits that he used to oppose gay marriage but has since come to believe it poses no threat to marriage or society and should thus be legalized. Does knowing that he used to oppose gay marriage but changed his mind influence your opinion of his argument? If so, in what way?

# Gay Marriage Is Bad for Children

## Toni Meyer

*"The social experiment of homosexual 'marriage' will cause serious harm to children."*

Gay marriage threatens children and puts them at risk for multiple harms, argues Toni Meyer in the following viewpoint. She cites research from a major study that showed children raised by gay as opposed to straight parents are more at risk for drug and alcohol use, rape or molestation, mental health problems, economic problems, and being homosexual themselves. Meyer thinks that children need both mothers and fathers in their lives; to intentionally deprive them of one or the other is unfair and damaging. Meyer concludes that gay marriage should not be legalized because of the harms it poses to children: It is unconscionable to make children suffer because of the desires of adults.

Meyer is the senior research analyst for the New Jersey Family Policy Council, a conservative group that opposes gay marriage.

### AS YOU READ, CONSIDER THE FOLLOWING QUESTIONS:

1. What point does Meyer make about speeding laws, orchestral standards, and gay marriage?
2. What, according to the author, did a study find to be a "characteristic mark" of gay relationships?
3. Who is Doug Mainwaring, as introduced by Meyer?

As the Supreme Court began hearing two important challenges to marriage law last week [in April 2013], the news has been filled with renewed arguments by some federal and state leaders to change the definition of marriage to include same-sex couples. Recent polls reporting increased public support for same-sex marriage have emboldened their push.

## Accommodating Gay Relationships

After years of emotional portrayals of same-sex relationships in TV sitcoms, movies and now in blatant advertising campaigns, a creeping cultural shift is taking place. A Pew Research poll indicated that the biggest reason 32 percent of those who changed their minds and now support same-sex "marriage" did so was that they know someone who is gay.

This change of heart comes from a sense of compassion for the individual, but marital ideals and standards that encourage society to aspire to the best possible outcomes cannot be abandoned to accommodate every individual. Speeding laws are not waived for the unfortunate soul who has to catch an important flight. Orchestral standards are not waived for the musician because he has devoted his or her life to studying an instrument and needs the job to support a family.

It is either right to maintain the ideal man-woman definition of marriage—our most important social institution—or it is not. We must not base our decision on compassion for gays (or misunderstood sense of fairness), whether the gay person is our child, a sibling, friend or anyone else.

## The Harm Done to Children

Same-sex couples in New Jersey already receive equal benefits under civil-union law, and these unions deserve distinction for good reason. A new gold-standard, peer-reviewed, family structures study released in June 2012 by sociology professor Mark Regnerus from the University of Texas indicates that the social experiment of homosexual "marriage" will cause serious harm to children. The study found that children raised by gay and lesbian parents are significantly more likely than those raised in a two-parent heterosexual home to: have social and mental health problems requiring therapy, identify themselves as homosexual, choose cohabitation, be unfaithful to partners, contract sexually transmitted diseases, be sexually molested or raped by a parent or adult, have lower income levels, drink to get drunk, and smoke tobacco and marijuana.

*The author believes that gay marriage should not be legalized because of the harm it poses to children, who, the author contends, should not be made to suffer just because adults desire to be together.*

# Is Gay Marriage Bad for Children?

Poll data analyzed by the Pew Research Center show that 35 percent of Americans consider it a bad thing when children are raised by gay and lesbian couples. The poll also found that 34 percent of respondents do not regard same-sex couples with children to meet the definition of a family.

**Percent saying increase in gay/lesbian couples raising children is . . .**

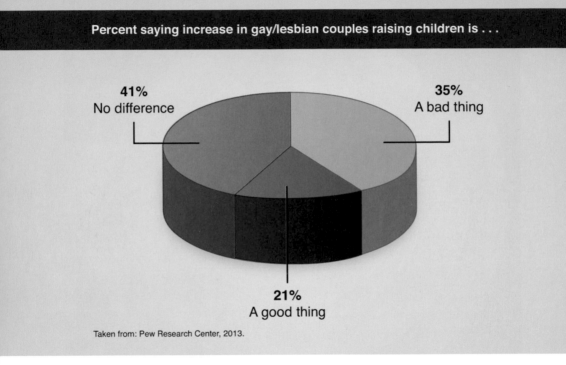

41%
No difference

35%
A bad thing

21%
A good thing

Taken from: Pew Research Center, 2013.

A key difference that sets this study above all others is that it uses a data set of 2,988 persons ages 18 to 39—including 175 adults raised by lesbian mothers and 73 adults raised by gay fathers—marking the first research from a new dataset, which initially included some 15,000 people. The research not only showed that there was a major difference between children from both groups, but highlighted that family instability is a "characteristic mark" of same-sex relationships.[1] Gay activists have criticized the study saying it compares gay families [many single gay parents] with 2-parent heterosexual families. While this is a factor, due to characteristics of gay relationships there are problems that will likely never be overcome in a statistically representative population study: gays represent just 2–3% of the population, only a minority of gay couples marry, and they break up at a significantly higher rate[2] than heterosexual couples.[3] Regardless, there are some pathologies higher among children raised by a same-sex parent even compared to a single heterosexual parent.[4] These poor life outcomes will require greater government tax dollar assistance and encourage more young people to accept and experiment with same-sex behavior.

## Gay Marriage Deprives Children

For those who believe changing the definition of marriage will not hurt their marriages, consider that the social mistakes we as a society have already made, and are headed toward now, will weigh most heavily on the shoulders of children. They are the innocent victims of social experimentation and have become morally and even physically broken in the name of so-called "freedom, equality and progress." Since 1994, the number of homosexual men has increased 18 percent, but the number of women who identify as such has gone up 157 percent.[5] This suggests there are strong cultural factors at work in encouraging same-sex behaviors, and at least indirectly, it undermines the whole theory of being "born that way."

This month, Doug Mainwaring, a gay man, wrote an insightful article for thepublicdiscourse .com,[6] sharing that intellectual honesty and experience as a gay person raising children can lead to opposing same-sex marriage. "There are perhaps a hundred different things, small and large, that are negotiated between parents and kids every week," he said. "Moms and dads interact differently with their children. To give kids two moms or two dads is to withhold . . . someone whom they desperately need and deserve in order to be whole and happy. It is to permanently etch 'deprivation' on their hearts."

> **FAST FACT**
>
> Legalized same-sex marriage began in Netherlands in 2001. Over the next few years, the rate of the country's children born out of wedlock rose from 25 percent in 2000 to 35 percent in 2005, according to statistics compiled by Eurostat.

## Children Must Come Before Adult Desires

A genderless union, with or without adoption, may be considered a family, but it is not a marriage. While similar in some ways, it is no more a marriage than a polygamous union and does not bring the same benefits to children or society that marriage brings.

New Jersey's gay activist organization Garden State Equality is launching a new campaign asking legislators to "vote their conscience" and override the governor's veto of a bill that would redefine marriage for all of us. Our conscience should always tell us to put children first, ahead of adult desires, and legislators have a responsibility to pursue public policy rooted in the well-being of all children.

**EVALUATING THE AUTHOR'S ARGUMENTS:**

In this viewpoint Toni Meyer relies on a study by Mark Regnerus to argue that gay marriage harms children. In the following viewpoint Bill Keller argues that the Regnerus study is deeply flawed and does not actually impart information about how children of same-sex couples fare. After reading both viewpoints, do you think the Regnerus study is valid? Can it alone be used to determine whether gay marriage harms children? Why or why not?

1. www.sciencedirect.com/science/article/pii/S0049089X12000610.
2. Gunnar Andersson et al., "The Demographics of Same-Sex Marriage in Norway and Sweden," Demography 43 [2006]: 79-98.) Divorce risk for gay men is 50 percent higher than for heterosexual couples and the divorce risk for partnerships of lesbian women is about double the rate compared to heterosexual couples.
3. A follow-up assessment of more recent Norwegian statistics, presented at the 2012 annual meeting of the Population Association of America (PAA), found no evidence that the gender gap in same-sex divorce has closed (Noack et al., 2012).
4. www.markregnerus.com/uploads/4/0/6/5/4065759/regnerus_response_to_critics_in_nov_2012_ssr.pdf p. 1369 (3 of 11).
5. www.gallup.com/poll/158066/special-report-adults-identify-lgbt.aspx.
6. Doug Mainwaring, "I'm Gay & I Oppose Same-Sex Marriage," March 3, 2013. www.thepublicdiscourse.com/2013/03/9432/.

**Viewpoint 4**

# It's About the Children

### Bill Keller

In the following viewpoint Bill Keller argues that gay marriage does not harm or disadvantage gay children. He cites numerous studies that show that socially, children of gay parents are at no significant disadvantage, and the children of same-sex couples are at an advantage compared with children raised by single parents. The only study that showed children to be harmed by gay marriage studied not necessarily gay relationships but failed heterosexual relationships. In Keller's opinion, this study is so deeply flawed, its findings are not credible or relevant to the heterosexual marriage debate. More damaging than same-sex marriage to children, says Keller, is when the law denies their parents the benefits of parenthood that are extended to opposite-sex couples. For example, children are harmed when their parents are unable to visit them in the hospital, or otherwise enjoy the benefits and stability that come along with marriage. Keller concludes that if conservatives truly wanted to help children, they would realize that legalized gay marriage offers children stability, legitimacy, and important rights and benefits.

Keller is a columnist for the *New York Times*.

> *"The research shows no significant disadvantage associated with being raised by lesbian mothers or gay fathers."*

**AS YOU READ, CONSIDER THE FOLLOWING QUESTIONS:**
  1. What, according to Keller, is the purpose of divorce laws?
  2. Why is it difficult to study the effect of same-sex unions on children, according to the author?
  3. What does Keller point out as true about the children of interracial marriages?

The defenders of traditional marriage tell us the argument is, first and foremost, about the children. You might not know that from the buzz surrounding the Supreme Court deliberations.[1] The children of gay and lesbian parents got a few splashes of attention, including a powerful endorsement of marriage equality from the 60,000-member American Academy of Pediatrics and one sympathetic-sounding aside from Justice Anthony Kennedy during the hearings. But for the most part, the debate has focused on the rights of grown-ups and the powers of states, not so much on the well-being of children. And when that subject does come up, the discussion is often shallow or misleading.

So let's talk about the children.

The stakes for children in this debate fall roughly into two categories. One is legal: A great scaffolding of laws and benefits created to keep children secure and loved is denied to children who grow up with parents of the same gender. Can that be solved without letting same-sex couples marry? The other is social: Researchers have attempted to ascertain whether kids who grow up with two moms or two dads fare differently from kids growing up with one of each. Is there any reason to think same-sex households are bad for children, and if so should policy makers tread carefully?

Take the legal question first.

## It Is Right to Recognize Parents as Parents

Nobody knows how the Supreme Court will rule, but the best guess of court-watchers is this: The justices will throw out the federal Defense of Marriage Act, assuring that married same-sex couples will be enti-

---

1. The author is referring to *United States v. Windsor* and *Hollingsworth v. Perry*, two gay marriage–related cases the Supreme Court heard in 2013.

tled to approximately the same treatment under federal law as other couples. But they seem likely to leave it up to the states to decide whether gays can get married in the first place.[2]

That means, first of all, that states can continue to deny children of homosexuals many safeguards that protect children of straight couples. The history of this issue is filled with stories of hardship and heartbreak befalling children whose parents are not recognized as—well, as parents. There are the cases of mothers and fathers turned away from a child's hospital bed because they are not "family." There are the cases of beloved adults denied visitation rights after a breakup. Many states restrict the ability of a gay parent to adopt or to respond to a child's medical emergency. Divorce laws were created in large part to assure that children get financial and emotional support when marriages end: no marriage, no divorce, no support.

It is true that a well-crafted civil union law—one that assures gay and lesbian partners the same spousal parenting rights as marriage—can help remedy these cruelties. But many states do not offer civil

> **FAST FACT**
>
> In a March 2013 policy paper, the American Academy of Pediatrics declared that it is in children's best interest for their same-sex parents to marry and that there is no evidence that such marriages hurt children.

unions at all. Among those that do, not all civil union laws are so rigorous; some are mere approximations of equality that do not confer full parental rights. [US Supreme Court] Justice Ruth Bader Ginsburg might refer to them as "skim-milk civil unions."

And civil unions do not address the stigma attached to being treated as if your family is not a "real" family—a stigma that amounts to an official imprimatur for bullying and humiliation. "Kids understand and internalize the sense that something is wrong with their families and that they should be ashamed," said Camilla Taylor of Lambda Legal, who has followed many of these cases through the courts.

2. The justices did rule this way in June 2013.

## Children of Gay Parents Have No Significant Disadvantages

Which brings us to the social question. Defenders of the status quo (including [US Supreme Court] Justice Antonin Scalia) would have you believe that the research on children growing up with gay parents is deeply ambiguous. If you spend time in the recent archives of such periodicals as *Pediatrics, Applied Developmental Science, Social Science Research* and the *Journal of Marriage and Family*, you will learn otherwise.

Taken one by one, the studies are far from perfect. The samples are usually small and not random. Few are "longitudinal"—that is, following subjects over years or decades. Social science rarely delivers conclusive results under the best circumstances, and with same-sex marriage researchers face particular handicaps. The number of children who have been raised entirely by stable, same-sex couples is relatively small. (According to the demographer Gary Gates of U.C.L.A. [University of California at Los Angeles], a majority of children being raised by gay or lesbian parents were born to opposite-sex couples who later broke up.) Homosexuality still encounters bigotry that makes potential study subjects wary. And it is hard to untangle all the variables in the raising of children.

But it is fair to say that the research shows no significant disadvantage associated with being raised by lesbian mothers or gay fathers—not in academic performance, not in psychological health, not in social or sexual development, not in violent behavior or substance abuse. And the research leaves little doubt that stable, two-parent households (of whatever flavor) are likely to be better off financially, more attentive to the upbringing of children and more secure than single-parent households.

## A Deeply Flawed Study

Of course, the burden of proof lies with opponents of marriage equality. In legal parlance, they are the ones who seek to establish a "governmental interest" that justifies discriminating against gay couples. So where's their evidence?

They lean heavily on one study published last year [in 2012] by Mark Regnerus, an associate professor of sociology at the University of Texas. He compared two groups of young adults. The first group told interviewers that at some point in their upbringing a parent experienced a same-sex "romantic relationship." In most cases, the parents subsequently broke up. In other words, this group wasn't the offspring of committed gay couples but of failed unions, some

*The author cites numerous studies that show that children raised by gay parents are at no significant social disadvantage, and that they even have an advantage over children raised by single parents.*

of them probably sham marriages. It's not even clear whether the parents who strayed were gay or lesbian, or simply experimenting. The second group consisted of kids who spent their childhoods in lasting, married, mom-and-dad families.

Guess which group had problems?

The study was pretty well demolished by peers. It may have confirmed the emotional toll of broken homes, but it said nothing much about growing up with gay parents. Regnerus, when I talked to him, conceded that his study compared apples and oranges, because "I didn't have oranges." He was unable to articulate what bearing his study had on gay marriage except that it "paints the reality of people's lives as fairly complicated."

## Rights Are Not Subject to Quality

Activists against same-sex marriage, however, are not all that particular about the quality of their evidence. They are happy to enlist and exaggerate dubious research to create the illusion that there is a scientific stalemate, and they often get away with it. When David Gregory of "Meet the Press" [televised news and interview program] brought up the fact that the American Academy of Pediatrics endorses marriage equality, Ralph Reed of Focus on [the] Family retorted, "And the American *College* of Pediatricians came out the other way." Nobody pointed out that this "college" is a tiny, conservative rump that broke away from the main pediatric group in 2002 over gay adoption. To quote its Web site, "The College bases its policies and positions upon scientific truth within a framework of ethical absolutes." Among its inviolable beliefs are "the sanctity of human life from conception to natural death and the importance of the fundamental mother-father family (female-male) unit in the rearing of children." Naturally, the college loves the Regnerus study.

Even if the research showed that children of same-sex couples were less well adjusted, which it does not, would we really want government to intervene? After all, there is research showing that children whose parents are of different races struggle more, on average, than children with parents of the same race. But no serious person suggests we turn back the clock on interracial marriage.

"It really doesn't matter very much what Regnerus or anybody else shows," concludes James Wright, the editor of the journal that published the Regnerus study and its critics. "It's a question of fundamental civil rights."

**EVALUATING THE AUTHOR'S ARGUMENTS:**

In this viewpoint Bill Keller argues that denying gay couples the legal framework in which to raise children damages them more than simply being raised by two people who are gay. What do you think? Are children harmed when they are raised by gay parents? Or are they harmed by being denied the benefits and rights that come along with having married parents? Explain your reasoning and use examples from the texts you have read.

# Chapter 3

# What Effect Would Gay Marriage Have on Society?

Some say gay marriage will ruin society; others say it will improve society.

# Gay Marriage Infringes on Religious Liberty

*"Advocates concerned with liberty and equality fought to open marriage to gay couples. . . . Here's hoping [they also] will defend the liberty of cultural conservatives to live their lives according to their faith."*

## Timothy P. Carney

Legalized gay marriage infringes on the religious values and liberty of other Americans, argues Timothy P. Carney in the following viewpoint. Carney discusses cases in which wedding vendors declined to provide services for gay weddings, claiming that participating in such an event violated their religious beliefs. The vendors were cited by authorities for having discriminated against people on the basis of their sexual orientation; Carney contends that such a citation amounts to a violation of the wedding vendors' religious rights. Carney says the state should not be allowed to compel people to accept unions that offend their religious and moral sensibilities. He maintains that allowing religious liberty is one of America's greatest attributes, and it is utterly anti-American to force people to violate their religious beliefs.

Carney is a senior columnist for the *Washington Examiner,* a conservative political magazine.

AS YOU READ, CONSIDER THE FOLLOWING QUESTIONS:
1. How much did Elaine Huguenin have to pay in damages for declining to photograph a lesbian wedding?
2. Who is Barronelle Stutzman, as described by the author?
3. Why specifically does Carney say the civil rights analogy cannot work for gay marriage?

Today's talk of tolerance and acceptance of gay marriage will soon give way to intolerance and rejection of those who hold a traditional view of marriage.

The next offensive in this culture war will involve wielding government to force individuals to accept the new definition of marriage, falsely invoking analogies to civil rights.

## Gay Marriage Prevents People from Living According to Their Values

As a prototype, consider the assault on the liberty of Elaine Huguenin, the wedding photographer in New Mexico. In 2006, a couple asked her to photograph their wedding. When she learned the couple were lesbians, she declined, explaining that pursuant to her faith, she only photographed man-woman weddings.

The couple got a different photographer, but they sued Huguenin. In New Mexico, there is no gay marriage.[1] In a recent poll, most New Mexicans said they oppose gay marriage. But the state outlaws discrimination based on sexual orientation.

The New Mexico Human Rights Commission found Huguenin had broken the law, and ordered her to pay $7,000. Huguenin, with the aide of the pro-bono civil liberties law firm Alliance Defense Fund, has sued and the case is now before the state Supreme Court.

Try to live your own life according to traditional values, and the state will come after you, and compel you to live according to its values.

Florist Barronelle Stutzman owns Arlene's Flowers in Richland, Wash. A gay man, who was a long-time customer of Arlene's, asked

---

1. The New Mexico Supreme Court ruled unanimously in December 2013, after this viewpoint was written, that denying gays the right to marry was unconstitutional, making New Mexico the seventeenth state to allow gay marriage.

Stutzman to arrange flowers for his wedding. She declined, citing her belief that marriage is a union between a man and woman. Now Washington Attorney General Bob Ferguson is coming after Stutzman, saying, in effect, she must participate in this gay wedding.

How does Ferguson justify using the power of the state to impose his morality? "If Ms. Stutzman sells flowers to heterosexual couples," the *Seattle Post-Intelligencer* quotes Ferguson saying, "she must sell them to same-sex couples."

But obviously Stutzman did sell flowers to same-sex couples, happily—that's why this particular client was a long-time customer. What she refuses to do is participate in a ceremony that the state calls marriage, but which she doesn't consider to be marriage.

*Florist Barronelle Stutzman (pictured) was sued by the state of Washington on behalf of a gay couple for refusing on moral grounds to provide flowers for a same-sex wedding.*

This is why the civil rights analogy doesn't work. Huguenin's case and Stutzman's case aren't about small businesswomen refusing to serve gay people. They are about businesswomen refusing to endorse the novel definition of marriage.

## Religious Liberty Is at Stake

Now that a majority of the U.S. Supreme Court has asserted that the only reason to object to gay marriage is to "demean" gay people, expect this offensive in the culture war to escalate.

President [Barack] Obama promised that he won't try to force churches to administer gay weddings. That's very kind of him. But Obama's contraception mandate [compelling insurance providers to pay for contraceptives] has shown us how narrowly he views religious liberty.

Maybe Obama or his successor won't use an executive order to rewrite the Sacrament of Holy Matrimony, but government will go after churches all the same. The Cardinal O'Boyle Hall that your parish occasionally rents to outside groups? Better allow gay wedding receptions there or face the wrath of the state.

> ## FAST FACT
>
> In New Jersey a Methodist organization that refused the use of its pavilion for a same-sex wedding had its tax exemption for the pavilion area revoked, costing it an estimated twenty thousand dollars.

You're allowed to be religious, of course, but only on the Sabbath. If you dare step into the world of commerce or public service, the government will impose its morality on you.

## The War on Religion

You see it in Obama's rhetoric: he talks of "freedom of worship" rather than freedom of religion. It's a push to bring to heel all rivals of government. Liberal writer Kevin Drum made it pretty explicit during the contraception mandate debate:

"I'm tired of religious groups operating secular enterprises (hospitals, schools)," he wrote, "hiring people of multiple faiths, serving

## Religion Is a Big Factor for Americans Against Same-Sex Marriage

A Gallup poll found that Americans who oppose the legalization of same-sex marriage, 43 percent of the adult population, are most likely to explain their position on the basis of religious beliefs and/or interpretation of biblical passages dealing with same-sex relations.

**Asked of those opposed to same-sex marriage: What are some of the reasons why you oppose legal same-sex marriages?**

| Reason | Percent |
| --- | --- |
| Religion/Bible says it is wrong | 47% |
| Marriage should be between a man and a woman | 20% |
| Morally wrong/Have traditional beliefs | 16% |
| Civil unions are sufficient | 6% |
| Unnatural/Against laws of nature | 5% |
| Undermines traditional family structure/Mother and father | 5% |
| Other | 7% |
| No opinion | 4% |

Taken from: *USA Today*/Gallup. November 26–29, 2012.

the general public, taking taxpayer dollars—and then claiming that deeply held religious beliefs should exempt them from public policy."

The thrust: religious groups should only do religion—they shouldn't feed the poor, clothe the naked, educate the young.

And individuals who adhere to religions? Leave your faith at the church door. The Obama administration has argued in the contraception mandate cases that we lose our freedom of conscience the second we enter into commerce with other people.

The Left has long been the aggressor in the culture war. The crushing power of government has long been their weapon.

Many politically involved writers and advocates concerned with liberty and equality fought to open marriage to gay couples. Now that they've won, here's hoping that those who care about liberty will defend the liberty of cultural conservatives to live their lives according to their faith.

## EVALUATING THE AUTHOR'S ARGUMENTS:

In this viewpoint Timothy P. Carney argues that offering marriage rights to same-sex couples takes away the rights of others to practice their religion in their day-to-day lives. Steve Chapman, in the following viewpoint, argues that same-sex marriage rights are infinite and limitless, meaning that they do not take away anything from anyone else. In your opinion, who is correct, and why? Cite at least one of the texts in your answer.

# Gay Marriage Is Not a Threat to Freedom

**Steve Chapman**

*"The only liberty [antigay religious groups] will lose is the liberty to deprive others of their liberty."*

Steve Chapman is a syndicated columnist for the *Chicago Tribune*. In the following viewpoint he argues that gay marriage does not infringe on religious liberty. He contends that same-sex marriage is truly a right because it is infinite—allowing same-sex couples to marry does not take away rights for others. Groups who claim that legalizing same-sex marriage infringes on their religious liberty have it wrong, maintains Chapman: All they are losing is their freedom to infringe on other people's freedom. He acknowledges there will be conflicts over how to logistically balance the religious liberty of people and organizations with the right of same-sex couples to marry, but these are small issues that will be worked out with time and in the courts. Chapman concludes that marriage rights do not infringe on anyone else's religious liberty, and the fear that they will is utterly irrational.

AS YOU READ, CONSIDER THE FOLLOWING QUESTIONS:
1 What did Thomas Jefferson write about freedom, according to Chapman?
2. On what issue does the author say the Supreme Court ruled in 2003?
3. Chapman says that employment discrimination laws have not been applied to what?

One reason Americans have moved so rapidly toward support of same-sex marriage is their stubborn bias toward liberty. When interest groups demand something material, or when they seek to take something from other groups, the public is apt to resist. But when a group asks to live and let live, it can usually count on getting its way.

## Gay Marriage Does Not Cost Opponents Anything

Legal scholars have long thought that if the Supreme Court upheld same-sex marriage, it would base that decision on the 14th Amendment's guarantee of "the equal protection of the laws." When Justice Anthony Kennedy made the case for overturning the Defense of Marriage Act [DOMA], though, he relied on a different provision. DOMA, he wrote, "is a deprivation of an essential part of the liberty protected by the Fifth Amendment."

> **FAST FACT**
>
> In 2012 the Public Religion Research Institute found that 59 percent of Catholics and 56 percent of white mainline Protestants favor the legalization of same-sex marriage.

The right to marry a person of the same sex fits perfectly within Thomas Jefferson's conception of freedom. "It does me no injury for my neighbor to say there are twenty gods or no God," he wrote. "It neither picks my pocket nor breaks my leg."

The beauty of gay marriage is that it grants something to one group that doesn't come at the expense of anyone else. Heterosexual rights are undisturbed. Straight people could marry before any state legalized same-sex matrimony, and likewise after.

That fact explains why so many non-gays have come to embrace the idea. But it presents a high hurdle for opponents of same-sex marriage. Even Americans who have moral qualms about it may not think the law should try to dictate morality.

*Thomas Jefferson wrote of religious freedom, "It does me no injury for my neighbor to say there are twenty gods or no God. It neither picks my pocket nor breaks my leg." Gay marriage proponents contend that same-sex marriages will not impinge on anyone's religious liberty.*

# Religion and Same-Sex Marriage Are Not Mutually Exclusive

Despite the conventional wisdom that religious people oppose same-sex marriage, a 2011 poll by the Public Religion Research Institute found the majority of nonaffiliated Christians, Catholics, and white mainstream Protestants are in favor of legalizing it.

## View on Same-Sex Marriage, by Religion

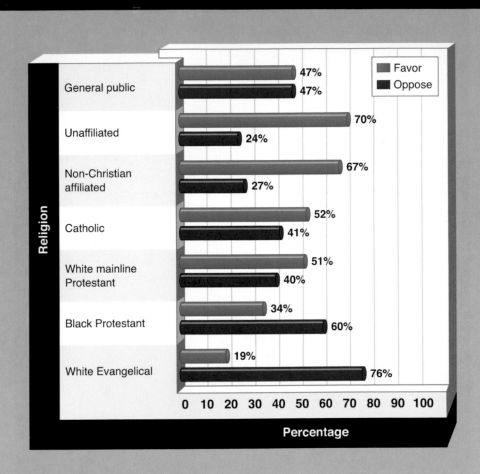

Taken from: Public Religion Research Institute; Millennials, Religion & Gay and Lesbian Issues Survey, July 2011.

After all, the Supreme Court said in 2003 the Constitution protects the freedom of adults to engage in sodomy—a decision that conservatives spent five minutes denouncing and never mentioned again. (Well, except for Attorney General Ken Cuccinelli of Virginia, who wants to reinstate its ban.) It's a small step from saying people should be free to have sex with whomever they want to saying they should be free to marry whomever they choose.

## Losing Focus on the Real Rights Violations

So how did staunch opponents of gay rights react to the decisions striking down DOMA while upholding marriage equality in California? By claiming that it would trample on *their* rights.

Thomas Peters, the communications director for the National Organization for Marriage, told me, "Same-sex marriage and religious freedom don't coexist very well. In fact, they probably are mutually exclusive."

Bryan Fischer of the American Family Association called the DOMA verdict "the greatest threat to the First Amendment in history." The Liberty Institute said the rulings will mean "attempts to use government to punish those who disagree" and "create a climate of fear and oppression."

It's a bit rich for these groups to complain that the court is infringing on their freedom to infringe on the freedom of gays. Advocates of same-sex marriage are not trying to exclude heterosexuals from matrimony. They are only asking to be free to practice it, as well.

## No One Is Free to Deprive Others of Freedom

But opponents charge that churches will be forced to host same-sex weddings and their clergy will be required to perform them. Churches that refuse, they say, may be stripped of their tax-exempt status.

The likelihood that any of these fears will come to pass ranges from minimal to zero. State laws allow divorce, but Catholic priests haven't been forced to preside at the weddings of divorced Catholics. Employment discrimination laws haven't been applied to end bans on female clergy. Nor have such internal church policies led to the loss of standard tax exemptions.

The only real friction comes in areas where religious institutions provide public accommodations or act as agents of government. A

Methodist organization in New Jersey lost a special tax break for an open-air pavilion after it refused to let a lesbian couple use it for a civil union ceremony. Catholic Charities abandoned the adoption business in Illinois rather than work with same-sex couples in civil unions.

Those cases may represent good or bad policy, but they're not a new thing. A hotel owner who objects to integration on religious grounds can't bar access to blacks. An organization taking state money for state contracts has to comply with state policies. Lawmakers will have plenty of these peripheral issues to argue about, but the idea that believers will suffer rank oppression is a fantasy.

The only liberty they will lose is the liberty to deprive others of their liberty. Sorry, but that's one freedom a free society doesn't offer.

**EVALUATING THE AUTHOR'S ARGUMENTS:**

In this viewpoint Steve Chapman argues that there is no conflict between religious liberty and same-sex marriage rights. In the previous viewpoint Timothy P. Carney says that such a conflict does exist. After reading both viewpoints, with which author do you agree, and why? Quote from the texts in your answer.

**Viewpoint**

**3**

# Why Gay Rights Are Civil Rights— and Simply Right

## David Lampo

*"Institutional homophobia in America . . . helps drive today's gay rights movement, just as institutional racism inspired and drove the civil rights movement."*

In the following viewpoint David Lampo likens the fight to legalize gay marriage to the 1960s civil rights movement for racial minorities. Lampo describes how for decades gay Americans were systematically discriminated against, legally persecuted, and physically and socially attacked. Viewed as sick and dangerous, gay people had to hide their sexual identities lest they be fired from their jobs, spied on by the government, socially discredited, beat up, and financially penalized. Lampo views the vast set of laws that have existed against homosexuality— ranging from the illegality of sending gay-related materials in the mail to prohibitions against sodomy, to the inability to marry— as similar to Jim Crow, the segregation laws that rendered black Americans second-class citizens. Lampo concludes that the right to marry is a civil right that no one should be denied, and thus he views the fight to legalize gay marriage as the civil rights cause of the present time.

Lampo is the author of the book *A Fundamental Freedom: Why Republicans, Conservatives, and Libertarians Should Support Gay Rights*. He is also the director of publications at the libertarian public policy organization the Cato Institute and a member of Log Cabin Republicans, a pro–gay rights Republican group.

## AS YOU READ, CONSIDER THE FOLLOWING QUESTIONS:

1. How did the American Psychiatric Association view homosexuality in the 1950s, as stated by Lampo?
2. How many people does Lampo say were fired from government jobs between 1947 and 1950 because of their suspected sexual orientation?
3. What right did the US Supreme Court affirm in 1958, according to the author?

There are many ways to define government's oppression of its citizens, and certainly many examples of it in U.S. history. And no doubt some government impositions on individual freedom have been broader than others or have had more widespread and deadlier consequences. Perhaps that was the point that James Antle intended to make in his recent article "Why Conservatives Say No" when he derided the comparison of the black civil rights struggle of the 20th century with the gay civil rights struggle of the 21st. "For liberals, every social issue is Selma," he wrote. "If you disagree with whatever social cause the liberal champions," he continued, "you are the new Hitler, or at least the new Bull Connor."

The widespread misconception today of gay people as mostly smug, well-off whites with fat bank accounts and comfortable (and, we're told, chosen) lifestyles, however, does not negate the undeniable history of often brutal treatment of gays and lesbians and their lack of basic human rights in the eyes of government for most of this nation's history.

The gay rights movement has made enormous strides over the past few decades, and the recent surge in public support for the once unthinkable concept of same-sex marriage reflects this quite radical shift in American culture. Homosexuality and support for the rights of gay and lesbian Americans are now widely accepted, even among Republicans, and a large majority of Americans say they know someone who is gay. But America was not always so accepting.

It was a very different story in the '50s and '60s, when gays and lesbians were still relatively invisible in American society. Many gays lived in ghettos of their own in major cities, and most lived their lives in the closet, concealing their sexual orientation to keep their jobs or prevent eviction. Few commercial establishments served openly gay customers, and many that catered to gay clientele, such as bars and restaurants, were owned or operated by organized crime, required to pay off police in order to operate what were often illegal establishments.

Police were rarely sympathetic to gay victims of assault and other violent crimes, and police themselves were often the perpetrators, raiding gay bars to close them or shake them down. Sodomy laws were on the books in every state except Illinois (after 1961), and some convicted of the crime were sentenced to long prison terms. The American Psychiatric Association (APA) listed homosexuality as a sociopathic personality disorder in 1951, and gays were routinely characterized in the media by crude stereotypes.

Because of the APA designation, 29 states had laws that allowed gays to be detained by the police simply on the suspicion they were gay. According to historian David Carter, sex offenders in California and Pennsylvania could be confined to mental institutes, and in seven states they could be castrated. Electroshock therapy and lobotomies were sometimes used to "cure" homosexuals in the '50s and '60s, and "in almost all states, professional licenses could be revoked or denied on the basis of homosexuality, so that professionals could lose their livelihoods," Carter writes in *Stonewall: The Riots That Sparked the Gay Revolution*.

Known gays and lesbians were forbidden from working for the federal government, and President Dwight Eisenhower formalized

> **FAST FACT**
>
> In 2012 the *Los Angeles Times* called gay rights the "fastest of all civil rights movements," because more than half of Americans now approve of gay marriage while 68 percent opposed it just sixteen years earlier.

*The author points to the US Ninth Circuit Court of Appeals' repudiation of the Don't Ask, Don't Tell policy of the military and asserts that it, like gay marriage, is not a civil rights issue.*

this policy of discrimination with an executive order in 1953. Those were the days of the Red Scare and fear of communist infiltration of the U.S. government, so the U.S. Senate and other official bodies routinely held hearings to investigate how many "sex perverts" worked for the feds since they were considered security threats. Between 1947 and 1950 alone, 1,700 federal job applicants were rejected, over 4,300 members of the armed forces were discharged, and 420 were fired from their government jobs simply for being gay or on the suspicion that they were gay.

The FBI and many police departments maintained lists of known and suspected homosexuals, and the U.S. Post Office actually kept track of addresses to which gay-related material was mailed. It was not until 1958 that the U.S. Supreme Court affirmed the right to send such material through the mail, ending the federal watchlist of such addresses.

In today's culture it's hard to believe such a time existed, but it was in that context of routine and widespread persecution of gay people that the modern gay civil rights movement was born in 1969 amid riots set off by police raids at a New York City gay bar called the Stonewall Inn. Not until the late 1970s and 1980s was routine police prosecution of gay people in most large cities ended. Only with the Supreme Court's *Lawrence* v. *Texas* decision in 2003 were state sodomy laws finally declared unconstitutional, and in spite of that decision some of those laws are still on the books, if rarely enforced. The prohibition against openly gay members serving in our armed forces ended less than three years ago with the repeal of Don't Ask, Don't Tell, and it will take years for that change to be fully implemented and accepted in military culture.

While gay and lesbian legal equality has vastly improved—the overturning of DOMA by the Supreme Court is just the latest example—workplace discrimination on the basis of sexual orientation is still widespread, and many state and local governments are not legally barred from practicing such discrimination. Most states prohibit not just marriage equality but any legal recognition of gay couples, and adoption by gay couples is illegal in most states. The legacy of virulent homophobia and legal inequality still looms large in many parts of this country, and will for many years to come.

Critics of gay marriage would be wise to learn the history of institutional homophobia in America and how it helps drive today's gay rights movement, just as institutional racism inspired and drove the civil rights movement. As I argue in my book *A Fundamental Freedom: Why Republicans, Conservatives, and Libertarians Should Support Gay Rights,* there is a fundamentally conservative and libertarian case for gay rights, including same-sex marriage, that is entirely consistent with the right's core principles of limited government and individual rights. Gay rights aren't just for liberals anymore: polls consistently show that even a majority of rank-and-file Republicans support most of the so-called "gay rights agenda"—as it's derisively called by its opponents—including some form of legal recognition for gay couples.

Conservatives will continue to debate the issues of gay rights and same-sex marriage for years, and many of them will come to understand the fundamental injustice of subjecting gay and lesbian Americans to their own form of Jim Crow rather than sharing in equal rights for all. But one thing that should be clear to all is the demonstrable history of homophobia in this country and why it continues to inspire today's movement for gay and lesbian equality.

## EVALUATING THE AUTHOR'S ARGUMENTS:

Viewpoint author David Lampo is a white man who is extremely sympathetic to the gay rights movement. Ellis Cose, author of the following viewpoint, is a black man who has devoted his life to exploring race relations in America. In what way does knowing their racial and professional backgrounds inform your opinion of their arguments about whether gay marriage constitutes the civil rights cause of the present time?

# Don't Compare Gay Rights, Civil Rights

*"There are similarities between the movement for racial equality and the movement for gay rights. . . . But in many respects, they are more different than they are alike."*

## Ellis Cose

The fight to legalize gay marriage cannot be compared to the civil rights movement, argues Ellis Cose in the following viewpoint. Cose concedes that the civil rights and gay rights movements share the goals of ending discrimination and prejudice, but Cose points out that the discrimination that black Americans faced, and continue to face, was and is so deeply entrenched in the American system that new generations continue to feel its effects even decades after laws were passed to eliminate such discrimination. Cose says this is not the case for gay Americans. Their ability to blend into society and the fact that prejudice against them does not carry over generation to generation, makes their struggle significantly less complex than the civil rights fight, which sought to end what Cose calls a racial caste system. Cose sympathizes with gay Americans and supports efforts to end prejudice against them, but thinks the struggle for gay marriage and other gay rights is fundamentally different than the ongoing struggle to achieve racial equality.

Cose writes frequently on race in the United States. He is the author of many important books on race, including *Rage of a Privileged Class* (1993) and *The End of Anger: A New Generation's Take on Race and Rage* (2011).

**AS YOU READ, CONSIDER THE FOLLOWING QUESTIONS:**
1. What, according to Cose, is "the legacy of subjugation"?
2. What does Cose say is fundamentally different about black and gay soldiers' experiences serving in the military?
3. What does the phrase "intergenerational transmission of disadvantage" mean, as the author uses it?

I t has become fashionable to wrap the gay rights movement in the mantle of America's earlier struggle for racial equality. As Sen. John McCain's [lesbian] daughter, Meghan, put it during one televised interview, "Gay marriage and everything having to do with the gay rights movement (is) my generation's civil rights issue." To make that assertion is not only to claim moral legitimacy but to invite comparison with the epic efforts that ultimately forced America to end its homegrown racial caste system.

Certainly, there are similarities between the movement for racial equality and the movement for gay rights. Both movements share the goals of ending discrimination and fostering decency. But in many respects, they are more different than they are alike. To point that out does not diminish the importance of the battle for equal treatment for gays. It merely acknowledges that each battle must be understood on its own terms.

## Black Americans Could Not Hide

Perhaps the most enduring lesson of the civil rights struggle is something that has little applicability to the fight for gay rights—and which also underscores its fundamental difference from it. And that has to do with the weight of history—with the legacy of subjugation that is not simply wiped away with the passage of prejudice and time. Decades after the civil rights movement proclaimed victory, blacks are still trapped in ghettos and prisons out of all proportion to their numbers. Black youngsters are much more likely than whites to be stuck in second-rate schools—or in lower tracks in decent schools—and to face a future of joblessness or marginal employment. The obstacles gays face are somewhat different.

In some sense, the "don't ask, don't tell" program makes the difference clear. The thoroughly discredited policy (most recently repudiated by the 9th U.S. Circuit Court of Appeals [and repealed by Congress about a month after this article appeared]) essentially ordered gay soldiers to stay closeted—to "pass," in other words, for straight. That would have been roughly equivalent, in racially segregated times, to demanding that black would-be soldiers "pass" for white. And many blacks did pass for white. But most could not. The racial markers were evident enough that, for most people, there was no hiding from the American system of classification. One's racial identity, for the most part, was as clear as the nose on one's face. That ability to instantly and easily (albeit, imprecisely) categorize was one thing that made it possible to organize an entire society around the principle of racial difference. It also allowed the practice of racism to be relentlessly oppressive, as entire communities were cordoned off and disadvantage was handed down through generations.

## FAST FACT

According to the Illinois Family Institute, civil rights are specific rights afforded to people as humans, not because of feelings, orientations, or conduct. As such, it does not consider marriage to be a civil right.

## Gays Do Not Face the Same Structural Barriers

With gays, we are not looking at roped-off communities or at the intergenerational transmission of disadvantage. We are certainly looking at the workings of prejudice, which, in all its guises, ought to be condemned. But because that prejudice is not linked to a system of economic oppression that will leave gay communities permanently incapacitated, the lack of social acceptance faced by gays—and even the violence visited upon those identified as gay—will not necessarily haunt their descendants generations after attitudes begin to change. So

# Jim Crow Laws in the United States, Late 1800s

Jim Crow laws were established in many states in the late nineteenth century. They sanctioned segregation between blacks and whites in education, transportation, hospitals, prisons, and other areas. Some argue that prohibitions on gay marriage are not the same as Jim Crow, which was systematic and had effects that continue today.

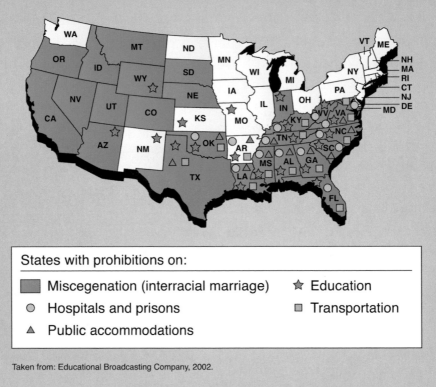

States with prohibitions on:

- Miscegenation (interracial marriage)   ★ Education
- O  Hospitals and prisons              ▢ Transportation
- △  Public accommodations

Taken from: Educational Broadcasting Company, 2002.

while the gay struggle is about changing attitudes, and laws that grew out of bigoted thinking, it is not about creating a pathway to opportunity (though gay marriage does confer certain economic rights) where none now exists.

The fight for racial equality was really two altogether different struggles. One was for tolerance and acceptance—and an end to socially sanctioned racial violence. That battle has essentially been won. The tougher battle, for removing structural barriers to opportunity, is far from over.

## A False Equivalency

When it comes to combating intolerance, the gay movement has much in common with the struggle for racial equality. And it can certainly draw hope from that struggle, which taught us that bigotry can be fought, that prejudice can fade—if not in one generation, in the next, provided that a society works at it. And clearly we are working at it. New York's recent [in 2011] sanctioning of same-sex marriage and Rhode Island's passage of a civil union bill are merely the latest signs of that.

This is not to say that certain communities should not work harder, including some conservative sectors of the black community, which have been hostile to gay appeals for acceptance. But as surely as the civil rights movement led to the mainstreaming of easily integrated blacks, the gay movement is leading to the mainstreaming of conventional-minded gays. And, eventually, we will look back, with slightly embarrassed bemusement, at the time when people seriously debated the morality of same-gender couples falling in love. We will chuckle that the U.S. government came up with anything as ridiculous as "don't ask, don't tell," and that we ever believed sexual orientation could tell us anything about another person's worth.

But that moment will not come any sooner by suggesting a false equivalency—or by arguing that the end of one movement has flowed naturally into another. It would be much more fruitful, I think, to ponder how the two movements can co-exist, and perhaps even reinforce each other, as they pursue their related, but also very different, goals.

## EVALUATING THE AUTHOR'S ARGUMENTS:

In this viewpoint Ellis Cose argues that prejudice against gays is fundamentally different from that against blacks, in part because of gay Americans' ability to blend into larger society. How do you think David Lampo, author of the previous viewpoint, would respond to this? Write two to three sentences on what you think he might say. Then, state your opinion—do you think the fact that gays can more easily hide their identity in larger society mitigates the extent of oppression against them? Why or why not?

**Viewpoint**

**5**

# Why Marriage Equality Is Good for the Economy and the Budget

*"All signs point to a positive economic impact from allowing gay men and lesbians to marry."*

**Bryce Covert**

In the following viewpoint Bryce Covert argues that legalized gay marriage would have a positive effect on federal and state economies in the following ways: Married gay couples would pay more in taxes, which could raise billions of dollars over the next decade. Being married would also allow many gay people to get health insurance and other benefits through their spouses, which would save the state from spending money to cover them through public assistance programs. States would raise significant amounts of money issuing marriage licenses and collecting taxes on sales related to the gay wedding industry and from wedding-related tourism. For all of these reasons the author concludes that gay marriage would have a positive economic effect everywhere it is legalized.

Bryce Covert, "Why Marriage Equality Is Good for the Economy and the Budget," ThinkProgress.org, June 26, 2013. This material "Why Marriage Equality Is Good for the Economy and the Budget" was created by the Center for American Progress Action (www.americanprogressaction.org). Reproduced by permission.

Covert is a journalist who covers economic issues for a variety of publications and websites, including ThinkProgress.org.

**AS YOU READ, CONSIDER THE FOLLOWING QUESTIONS:**
1. How much additional tax revenue does Covert say would have been collected by the federal government between 2011 and 2014 if gay marriage had been legal?
2. By how much would legalized gay marriage reduce annual spending on safety-net programs like Medicaid and Medicare, according to the author?
3. How much money does Covert report was generated by gay marriages in New York City after the state of New York legalized those marriages in 2011?

On Wednesday, the Supreme Court ruled that the Defense of Marriage Act, a federal law defining marriage as between a man and a woman, is unconstitutional while also dismissing the Proposition 8 case, effectively making it legal again for gay couples to get married in California.

These historic decisions mean so much to America's gay and lesbian couples. But they will also mean something for the federal budget and the economy at large. Without DOMA, the federal government will now give gay couples who are legally married in their home states benefits they had previously been denied. Those getting married in California will have an impact too.

In 2004, the Congressional Budget Office (CBO) looked at what it would mean for the federal government to recognize same-sex marriages. In all, this would impact 1,138 statutory provisions in which marriage is a factor in

> **FAST FACT**
>
> Before gay marriage became legal in December 2012, a January study that year by the Williams Institute at the University of California at Los Angeles estimated that if Washington state allowed gays to marry, gay weddings would bring in an estimated $57 million for the state in the first year alone.

# The Gay Wedding Economy

A 2012 study estimated that extending marriage to same-sex couples in just three states would generate over $166 million in wedding spending in the first three years alone.

| State | Number of Same-Sex Couples | Estimated Total Wedding Spending in First Three Years if 50 Percent of Same-Sex Couples Marry (Millions) |
|-------|---------------------------|------------------------------------------------------------------------------------------------------------|
| Maine | 3,958 | $15.5 |
| Maryland | 12,538 | $62.6 |
| Washington | 19,003 | $88.5 |
| **Total** | **35,499** | **$166.6** |

Taken from: Williams Institute, 2012.

determining benefits, including perhaps most prominently Social Security and federal taxes. The CBO found a slightly positive impact on the budget if same-sex marriages were to be legalized in all states and recognized by the federal government: an extra $1 billion each year for the next ten years. It estimates that the government would see a small increase in tax revenues: $500 million to $700 million annually from 2011 to 2014 depending on the fate of the Bush tax cuts (which were law at the time of the report).

The government would have to spend more on Social Security and the Federal Employees Health Benefits program, but it would also save money when it came to safety net programs such as Supplemental Security Income, Medicaid, and Medicare. On net, gay marriage would reduce spending by about $100 million to $200 million a year from 2010 to 2014.

The savings in programs that help low-income families come from the fact that gay and lesbian couples are more likely to live in poverty. As Matt Yglesias has written at *Slate*, a study from the Williams

Institute at UCLA found that 7.6 percent of lesbian couples live in poverty, compared to 5.7 percent of married opposite-sex couples. It also found that nearly a quarter of children living with a male same-sex couple and just under 20 percent of those living with a female same-sex couple live in poverty, compared to just 12.1 percent of children living with married heterosexual couples. This means they're more likely to rely on government benefits: 2.2 percent of women in lesbian couples receive cash assistance, versus 0.8 percent of women in opposite-sex couples, with a similar difference for men. Marriage reduces the likelihood that couples live in poverty and comes with important financial benefits.

States would also see a substantial benefit. A 2009 report on marriage equality in Maine found that allowing same-sex couples to marry would increase the state budget by $7.9 million a year, a substantial sum on the state level. This comes not just from an increase in income tax revenue when couples file jointly—$69,110 per year—but also an estimated $60 million spent on weddings and tourism over three years, which could generate $3.1 million in sales tax revenue, and

*A caterer prepares food for a gay wedding. The Congressional Budget Office found that if same-sex marriages were legalized in all states and recognized by the federal government it would generate an extra $1 billion in revenues each year for the next ten years.*

$538,193 in marriage license fees over three years.

In fact, a year after New York passed the Marriage Equality Act, gay marriages generated $259 million in economic impact in New York City alone.

On the business side, a report from the Human Rights Campaign found that while employers will likely have to pay more for benefits, they will have a negligible impact on costs. "In fact, because same-sex couples make up such a small percentage of the U.S. population," it notes, "the business benefits costs of allowing same-sex couples to marry will be no greater than the costs caused by fluctuations in the U.S. heterosexual marriage rates."

The Supreme Court decisions in no way guaranteed the ability for same-sex couples to get married in all 50 states, so many of the economic benefits are yet to be realized. But with DOMA struck down and 13 states legally allowing gay marriage, including California after the Proposition 8 ruling, the impacts are still likely to be felt in government coffers at both the federal and state level. All signs point to a positive economic impact from allowing gay men and lesbians to marry the people they love.

## EVALUATING THE AUTHOR'S ARGUMENTS:

In this viewpoint Bryce Covert suggests that legalized gay marriage could save governments money. Do you think the author provides enough evidence to convince him or her that legalizing gay marriage would benefit governments greatly? Why? List at least two pieces of evidence that swayed you.

# Facts About Gay Marriage

Editor's note: These facts can be used in reports to add credibility when making important points or claims.

According to the Universal Declaration of Human Rights adopted by the United Nations, the family unit is a fundamental part of society that is entitled to protection, and all people have the right to marry and to start a family.

*USA Today* notes that it is difficult to estimate how many same-sex couples are in the United States because states differ in the ways they collect statistics.

The Pew Research Center claims that polls and studies underestimate the number of gay people in the country because respondents are not comfortable with honestly reporting their sexual orientation.

Using US Census Bureau data, the Williams Institute at the University of California at Los Angeles (UCLA) estimates there are 114,100 legally married same-sex couples.

## Facts About Gay Marriage and the Law

According to the Pew Research Center, as of March 2014 gay marriage was legal in seventeen states and the District of Columbia:

- California
- Connecticut
- Delaware
- Hawaii
- Illinois
- Iowa
- Maine
- Maryland
- Massachusetts

- Minnesota
- New Hampshire
- New Jersey
- New Mexico
- New York
- Rhode Island
- Vermont
- Washington
- District of Columbia

Same-sex civil unions or domestic partnerships were permitted in:

- Colorado
- Nevada
- Oregon
- Wisconsin

According to CNN, gay marriage was explicitly banned in thirty-three states by March 2014.

According to the organization Freedom to Marry:

- The US General Accountability Office has identified over eleven hundred federal protections, rights, and responsibilities accorded to married couples but denied to unmarried partners. These include:

  - *Death benefits:* If a couple is unmarried and one partner dies without leaving a will, the other is not entitled to bereavement leave from work, to file wrongful death claims, to receive the partner's Social Security benefits, or to automatically inherit a home the decedent owned but shared with his or her partner.
  - *Health:* Unmarried partners are usually not considered next of kin for hospital visitation and in making emergency medical decisions.
  - *Parenting:* Only spouses are automatically granted the right to joint parenting, adoption, and visitation for nonbiological parents. Children of unmarried couples are not guaranteed child support or a legal relationship to both parents.

- *Divorce:* Unmarried partners who separate are not covered by laws pertaining to shared property, child support, and alimony.
- *Insurance:* Unmarried couples are often unable to receive joint home and auto insurance. Many employers offer health insurance to employees' legal spouses only.
- *Taxes:* Unmarried couples cannot file joint tax returns or receive tax benefits that married couples do.
- *Legal proceedings:* Only legal spouses are protected against having to testify against each other in judicial proceedings.

## Facts About Gay Marriage and Children

According to the American Association for Marriage and Family Therapy:

- In the United States between 1 million and 9 million children have at least one parent who is lesbian or gay.
- The 2000 US Census Bureau reported approximately 594,000 same-sex partner households. About 27 percent of these included children.
- Most children of same-sex couples are the biological offspring of one of the parents.
- A comprehensive study discovered that children with two moms or two dads fare just as well as other children in emotional functioning, sexual orientation, stigmatization, behavior, learning, and grade point averages.
- Adolescents with gay or lesbian parents reported feeling more connected at school than other kids.
- Children in same-gender households are more likely to talk about emotionally difficult topics and become more resilient, compassionate, and tolerant than children in straight homes.
- Same-sex families may face challenges that heterosexual families do not, including social stigma, dealing with extended family members who may criticize same-sex relationships/parenting, and lack of support from the other biological parent of their children.

Harvard University's Shorenstein Center has collected and reviewed these studies on its website:

- a 2009 study by University of Amsterdam and New York State Psychiatric Institute that found that children of lesbians were just as well adjusted, felt less parental pressure to conform to gender stereotypes, and were more uncertain about being heterosexual as compared to other kids;

- a Stanford University study published in 2010 that found that children of same-gender couples are as likely to make normal progress in school as other kids;
- a study in *Pediatrics* that reviewed over thirty years of research that showed that children's well-being is affected much more by their relationships with their parents than by the gender or sexual orientation of their parents and that denying same-gender couples the ability to marry increases families' stress and hurts their health and welfare; and
- a 2010 study published in *Pediatrics* that showed that seventeen-year-old daughters and sons of lesbian mothers rated significantly higher in social, academic, and total competence and significantly lower in social problems, rule-breaking, and aggression than others of the same age.

According to the Family Research Council, a Christian organization that promotes the traditional family, legalizing gay marriage would mean that

- schools would teach that gay relationships are equal to heterosexual ones;
- fewer children would be raised by a married mother and father, and more would be raised in permanently motherless or fatherless families and that growing up without a father may make young boys more likely to be incarcerated and adolescent girls more likely to get pregnant;
- more children would be conceived via sperm donation and that the children of sperm donors do not fare as well as other kids; and
- there would be little incentive for procreation, which is what defines marriage as a male-female union, and that same-gender marriage leads to lower birth and fertility rates.

The Christian legal group Liberty Counsel asserts that same-sex marriage hurts families because

- only heterosexual unions can produce children;
- kids need a mother and a father;
- mothers and fathers contribute different, important aspects of raising children; and

• kids who are not raised in a mother-father home tend to fare worse later in life.

## Opinions About Gay Marriage

According to Pew Research Center polls conducted in 2013,

- 87 percent of respondents know someone who is gay or lesbian, up from 61 percent in 1993;
- 49 percent say a close family member or close friend is gay or lesbian;
- 23 percent know "a lot" of gays or lesbians;
- 31 percent know a gay or lesbian who is raising children; and
- 45 percent think engaging in homosexual behavior is a sin whereas 45 percent say it is not.

In a 2004 *Los Angeles Times* poll,

- 60 percent of Americans said they would be upset if they had a child who identified as homosexual; today, 40 percent say they would be upset if they had a gay child;
- of 1,197 lesbian, gay, bisexual, and transgender (LGBT) respondents, 60 percent are currently married or would like to get married, compared with 76 percent of adults in the general population; and
- of unmarried LGBT respondents, 52 percent would like to marry in the future; 33 percent were unsure, and 15 percent said they do not want to marry.

According to a *Huffington Post*/YouGov poll in 2013,

- the Defense of Marriage Act prevents the federal government from recognizing same-gender marriages, even in states where they are legal. According to the survey, 41 percent of Americans said the Supreme Court should overturn it and 45 percent said it should uphold it;
- 41 percent of Americans said the Supreme Court should overturn it, and 45 percent said it should uphold it;
- 52 percent of Americans under age thirty assert that the federal government should recognize gay and lesbian marriages, while 37 percent oppose legalization at the federal level; and
- only 33 percent of those over age sixty-five said the federal government should legalize same-sex marriage, while 55 percent said it should not.

# Organizations to Contact

The editors have compiled the following list of organizations concerned with the issues debated in this book. The descriptions are derived from materials provided by the organizations. All have publications or information available for interested readers. The list was compiled on the date of publication of the present volume; the information provided here may change. Be aware that many organizations take several weeks or longer to respond to inquiries, so allow as much time as possible for the receipt of requested materials.

**American Civil Liberties Union (ACLU)**
125 Broad St., 18th Fl.
New York, NY 10004
(212) 944-9800
website: www.aclu.org

The ACLU is the nation's oldest and largest civil liberties organization. Its Lesbian and Gay Rights/AIDS Project, started in 1986, handles litigation, education, and public policy work on behalf of gays and lesbians, and it supports the legalization of same-sex marriage.

**Canadian Lesbian and Gay Archives**
PO Box 699, Station F
50 Charles St. East
Toronto, ON M4Y 2N6
Canada
(416) 777-2755
website: http://clga.ca

This organization collects and maintains information and materials relating to the gay and lesbian rights movement in Canada and elsewhere. Its collection of records and other materials documenting the stories of lesbians and gay men and their organizations in Canada is available to the public for education and research. It also publishes an annual newsletter, *Lesbian and Gay Archivist.*

**Children of Gays and Lesbians Everywhere (COLAGE)**
3543 Eighteenth St., Ste. 1
San Francisco, CA 94110
(415) 861-5437 • fax: (415) 255-8345
e-mail: colage@colage.org
website: www.colage.org

This organization provides support and advocacy for daughters and sons of lesbian, gay, bisexual, and transgender parents. Its website contains numerous reports, pamphlets, and other pieces of information.

**Concerned Women for America (CWA)**
1015 Fifteenth St. NW, Ste. 1100
Washington, DC 20005
(202) 488-7000
e-mail: mail@cwfa.org
website: www.cwfa.org

The CWA is an educational and legal defense foundation that seeks to strengthen the traditional family by promoting Judeo-Christian moral standards. It opposes gay marriage and the granting of additional civil rights protections to gays and lesbians. The CWA publishes the monthly magazine *Family Voice* and various position papers on gay marriage and other issues.

**Courage**
c/o Church of St. John the Baptist
210 W. Thirty-First St.
New York, NY 10001
(212) 268-1010 • fax: (212) 268-7150
e-mail: nycourage@aol.com
website: http://couragerc.net

Courage is a network of spiritual support groups for gay and lesbian Catholics who wish to lead celibate lives in accordance with Roman Catholic teachings on homosexuality. It publishes listings of local groups, a newsletter, and an annotated bibliography of books on homosexuality.

**Family Research Council (FRC)**
801 G St. NW
Washington, DC 20001
(800) 225-4008
website: www.frc.org

The council is a research, resource, and educational organization that promotes the traditional family, which it defines as a group of people bound by marriage, blood, or adoption. It opposes gay marriage and gay adoption rights and publishes numerous reports from a conservative perspective on issues affecting the family, including homosexuality and same-sex marriage.

**Family Research Institute (FRI)**
PO Box 62640
Colorado Springs, CO 80962-0640
(303) 681-3113
website: www.familyresearchinst.org

The FRI distributes information about family, sexuality, and substance abuse issues. It believes that strengthening heterosexual marriage would reduce many social problems, including crime, poverty, and sexually transmitted diseases. The institute publishes the bimonthly newsletter *Family Research Report* as well as numerous position papers and opinion articles. It opposes same-sex marriage.

**Focus on the Family**
8605 Explorer Dr.
Colorado Springs, CO 80995
(800) 232-6459
website: www.family.org

Focus on the Family is a conservative Christian organization that promotes traditional family values and gender roles. Its publications include the monthly magazine *Focus on the Family* and the numerous anti–gay marriage reports and articles.

**Gay and Lesbian Advocates and Defenders (GLAD)**
30 Winter St., Ste. 800
Boston, MA 02108
(617) 426-1350
website: www.glad.org

This is New England's leading legal rights organization. It is dedicated to ending discrimination based on sexual orientation, HIV status, and gender identity and expression. GLAD was a major supporter of same-sex marriage legalization in Connecticut, Massachusetts, New Hampshire, Maine, and Vermont.

**Howard Center for Family, Religion, and Society**
934 N. Main St.
Rockford, IL 61103
(815) 964-5819
website: www.profam.org

The purpose of the Howard Center is to provide research and understanding that demonstrates and affirms the traditional family and religion as the foundation of a virtuous and free society. The center believes that the natural family is the fundamental unit of society. The primary mission of the Howard Center is to provide a clearinghouse of useful and relevant information to support families and their defenders throughout the world. The center publishes the monthly journal *Family in America* and the *Religion and Society Report.*

**Lambda Legal Defense and Education Fund Inc.**
120 Wall St., 19th Fl.
New York, NY 10005
(212) 995-8585
website: www.lambdalegal.org

Lambda Legal is a public-interest law firm committed to achieving full recognition of the civil rights of homosexual persons. The firm addresses a variety of areas, including equal marriage rights, the military, parenting and relationship issues, and domestic-partner benefits. It publishes the quarterly *Lambda Update* and the pamphlet *Freedom to Marry.*

**National Center for Lesbian Rights**
870 Market St., Ste. 570
San Francisco, CA 94102
(415) 392-6257
website: www.nclrights.org

The center is a public-interest law office that provides legal counseling and representation for victims of sexual-orientation discrimination. Primary areas of advice include child custody and parenting, employment, housing, the military, and insurance. The center has a section devoted to marriage rights for lesbians and gays.

**National Gay and Lesbian Task Force (NGLTF)**
1325 Massachusetts Ave. NW, Ste. 600
Washington, DC 20005
(202) 393-5177
website: www.ngltf.org

The NGLTF is a civil rights–advocacy organization that lobbies Congress and the White House on a range of civil rights issues. The organization is working to make same-sex marriage legal. It publishes numerous papers and pamphlets, and the booklet *To Have and to Hold: Organizing for Our Right to Marry* and the fact sheet "Lesbian and Gay Families."

**National Organization for Marriage**
2029 K St. NW, Ste. 300
Washington, DC 20006
(888) 894-3604
e-mail: contact@nationformarriage.org
website: www.nationformarriage.org

This organization's mission is to protect marriage and the religious communities that sustain it. It was founded in 2007 in response to the growing movement to legalize same-sex marriage in state legislatures. It publishes numerous fact sheets, reports, and other articles on why same-sex marriage should not be legalized.

**The Rockford Institute Center on the Family in America**
928 N. Main St.
Rockford, IL 61103
(815) 964-5811
website: www.chroniclesmagazine.org/rockford-institute

The Rockford Institute works to return America to Judeo-Christian values and supports traditional roles for men and women. As such, it opposes same-sex marriage. Numerous articles on this and other issues are found in the institute's flagship publication, *Chronicles* magazine.

**Traditional Values Coalition**
139 C St. SE
Washington, DC 20003
(202) 547-8570
website: www.traditionalvalues.org

The coalition strives to restore what the group believes are traditional moral and spiritual values in American government, schools, media, and the fiber of American society. It believes that gay rights threaten the family unit and extend civil rights beyond what the coalition considers appropriate limits. The coalition publishes the quarterly newsletter *Traditional Values Report,* as well as various information papers, several of which specifically address same-sex marriage.

# For Further Reading

## Books

Badgett, M.V. Lee. *When Gay People Get Married: What Happens When Societies Legalize Same-Sex Marriage.* New York: New York University Press, 2009. The author examines gay marriage's potential impact in the United States by using data from European countries, specifically Netherlands, where same-sex couples have had the right to marry since 2001.

Bernstein, Mary, and Verta Taylor, eds. *The Marrying Kind? Debating Same-Sex Marriage Within the Lesbian and Gay Movement.* Minneapolis: University of Minnesota Press, 2013. Lesbian and gay voices speak on the desirability, viability, and social consequences of same-sex marriage.

Blankenhorn, David. *The Future of Marriage.* New York: Encounter, 2009. The author argues that if gay marriage is legalized, marriage as an institution will be so emptied of meaning that it will become a gender-neutral institution, rather than the premier gender-based institution of society.

Corvino, John, and Maggie Gallagher. *Debating Same-Sex Marriage.* New York: Oxford University Press, 2012. John Corvino (a philosopher and prominent gay advocate) and Maggie Gallagher (a nationally syndicated conservative columnist and cofounder of the National Organization for Marriage) debate what marriage is for, why the government sanctions it, how same-sex marriage affects children, and a host of other issues related to the topic.

Eskridge, William N., Jr., and Darren R. Spedale. *Gay Marriage: For Better or for Worse? What We've Learned from the Evidence.* New York: Oxford University Press, 2007. The authors use Scandinavia's sixteen-year history of legal registered partnerships as a basis for reflection on gay marriage in the United States.

Girgis, Sherif, Ryan T. Anderson, and Robert P. George. *What Is Marriage? Man and Woman: A Defense.* New York: Encounter,

2012. The authors argue that redefining civil marriage is unnecessary, unreasonable, and contrary to the common good.

Polikoff, Nancy D. *Beyond (Straight and Gay) Marriage: Valuing All Families Under the Law.* Boston: Beacon, 2009. A lawyer argues that the law's narrow definitions of family and marriage no longer work in today's society.

Rauch, Jonathan. *Gay Marriage: Why It Is Good for Gays, Good for Straights, and Good for America.* New York: Times/Henry Holt, 2004. A leading Washington journalist argues that gay marriage is the best way to preserve and protect society's most essential institution.

Streitmatter, Rodger. *Outlaw Marriages: The Hidden Histories of Fifteen Extraordinary Same-Sex Couples.* Boston: Beacon, 2013. Streitmatter explores the history of gay marriage prior to its development as a hot-button political issue.

Wolfson, Evan. *Why Marriage Matters: America, Equality, and Gay People's Right to Marry.* New York: Simon & Schuster, 2004. The author argues that marriage is a civil right that should be extended to gay couples.

## Periodicals and Internet Sources

Anderson, Ryan T. "Civil Rights and Marriage," *The Foundry* (blog), Heritage Foundation, June 20, 2013. http://blog.heritage.org.

Backholm, Joseph. "Is Gay Marriage a Civil Right?," Family Policy Institute of Washington, September 20, 2012. www.fpiw.org.

Blankenhorn, David. "How My View on Gay Marriage Changed," *New York Times,* June 22, 2012.

Cooke, Charles C.W. "Is Gay Parenting Bad for the Kids?," *National Review,* June 10, 2012.

Coontz, Stephanie. "Gay Marriage Isn't Revolutionary. It's Just the Next Step in Marriage's Evolution," *Washington Post,* January 7, 2011.

Douglas, Chuck. "States Should Decide on Gay Marriage," *Keene (NH) Sentinel,* May 16, 2013.

Frank, Nathaniel. "When the Facts Don't Matter," *Slate,* March 7, 2012. www.slate.com.

Goodman, Melissa. "Gay Marriage No Threat to Religious Rights," American Civil Liberties Union of New York State, July 10, 2011. www.nyclu.org.

Greenfield, Kent. "The Slippery Slope to Polygamy and Incest," *American Prospect,* July 15, 2013.

Hinkle, A. Barton. "Gay Marriage Should Lead to More Freedom, Not More Government Control," *Reason*, July 15, 2013.

Hunter, Jack. "Why Gay Marriage Isn't the '60s Civil Rights Fight," *American Conservative,* April 1, 2013.

Huntsman, John. "Marriage Equality Is a Conservative Cause," *American Conservative,* February 21, 2013.

Jones, Ed. "Don't Equate Gay Rights with Civil Rights of Blacks," *Colorado Springs Gazette,* February 27, 2013.

Keenen, Jillian. "Legalize Polygamy: Marriage Equality for All," *Slate*, April 15, 2013. www.slate.com.

Kerry, John. "Politicians Have the Right to Evolve on Gay Marriage," *Boston Globe,* July 10, 2011.

Klarman, Michael. "Why Gay Marriage Is Inevitable," *Los Angeles Times*, February 12, 2012.

Lee, Jia Hui. "Marriage Might Be the End of the Gay Community," Feminist Wire, March 31, 2013. http://thefeministwire.com.

McArdle, Megan. "Why Gay Marriage Will Win, and Sexual Freedom Will Lose," Daily Beast, March 26, 2013. www.thedailybeast.com.

Morse, Jennifer Roback. "When You Say 'Gay Marriage Is Inevitable,' Do You Mean Rich People Want It?," *American Thinker,* May 9, 2013. www.americanthinker.com.

Paltrow-Krulwich, Sam. "Marriage Equality Is About Civil Rights—and Tax Justice," City Watch (Los Angeles), April 5, 2013. http://citywatchla.com.

Ramsey, Bruce. "Supreme Court Should Let Each State Decide Same-Sex Marriage," *Seattle Times,* March 26, 2013.

Regnerus, Mark. "Gay Parents: Are They Really No Different?," *Slate*, June 11, 2012. www.slate.com.

Royster, Amber. "Don't Let Voters Decide Legality of Same-Sex Marriage," *Albuquerque (NM) Journal,* July 11, 2013.

Sprigg, Peter. "Same-Sex Marriage Is Contrary to the Public Interest," *Baltimore Sun,* February 1, 2011.

Sprigg, Peter. "The Top-Ten Harms of Same-Sex 'Marriage,'" Family Research Council, 2011. http://downloads.frc.org.

Staley, Peter. "Gay Marriage Is Great, but How About Some Love for the AIDS Fight?," *Washington Post,* June 28, 2013.

Tobia, Jacob. "Gay Marriage 2013: It's Not the End-All for the LGBT Rights Movement," Policymic.com. www.policymic.com.

Tushnet, Mark. "Our Rights, Not the Court's," *Wall Street Journal,* June 28, 2013.

## Websites

**The Human Rights Campaign's Marriage Center** (www.hrc.org /campaigns/marriage-center). This site collects and displays useful information about state ballot initiatives concerning same-sex marriage.

**The Pew Research Center's Gay Marriage and Homosexuality Page** (www.pewresearch.org/topics/gay-marriage-and-homosexuality). This site contains numerous studies conducted by the Pew Research Center about various topics related to gay marriage and homosexuality. Collected all in one place, this page makes for an excellent resource for reports, debate material, and research.

# Index

reasons for opposition to, *81*
should not be legal, 20–25
support for, by religious affiliation, *86*
voters should decide on legality of, 26–32
weakens institution of marriage, 54–58
Scalia, Antonin, 72
Serwer, Adam, 13
State(s)
    allowing same-sex marriage, *102*
    banning gay marriage are thriving, 51
    Jim Crow laws by, *98*
    numbers banning gay marriage, 22
    policies on gay unions by, *50*
    same-sex marriage is good for economies of, 100–104
    views on gay marriage as issue for, 29, *31*
*Stonewall* (Carter), 91
Stutzman, Barronelle, 78–80, *79*
Sullivan, Andrew, 61
Surveys
    on gay marriage as federal *vs.* state decision, *31*
    of gay people, on interest in marrying, 8
    on impact of gay marriage on children, *66*
    on inevitability of legal gay marriage, *42,* 43
    on knowing gay individual and change in support of gay marriage, 64
    on marriage status of US adults in 1960 *vs.* 2008, *56*

on reasons for opposing same-sex marriage, *81*
on support for same-sex marriage, 15, *31,* 43

T
Taylor, Camilla, 71
*Texas, Lawrence v.* (2003), *36,* 93
Trollope, Anthony, 61–62

U
*United States v. Windsor* (2013), *36,* 44, 60
US Constitution
prevents states from perpetuating inequality, 34–35
*See also* Fifth Amendment; Fourteenth Amendment

V
*Virginia, Loving v.* (1967), 14, 15, 35–37

W
*Wade, Roe v.* (1973), 16–17
Walker, Vaughn, 16, 17
West, Sonja, 12
*Why Conservatives Say No* (Antle), 90
Williams Institute, 102–103
*Windsor, United States v.* (2013), *36,* 44, 60
Wright, James, 75
Wydra, Elizabeth B., 33

Y
Yglesias, Matt, 102

# Picture Credits

© AP Images/Manuel Balce Ceneta, 23, 92

© AP Images/John Froschauer, File, 48

© AP Images/Eric Risberg, 103

© AP Images/Elaine Thompson, 16

© AP Images/The Tri-City Herald, Kai-Huei Yau, 79

© Gale, Cengage Learning, 31, 36, 42, 50, 56, 66, 81, 86, 98, 102

© Peter Horree/Alamy, 85

© Gina Kelly/Alamy, 53

© Carolyn A. McKeone/Science Source, 73

© Thomas J. Peterson/Alamy, 11

© Queerstock, Inc./Alamy, 65, 76

© Stock Connection Distribution/Alamy, 57

© Mark Wilson/Getty Images, 28, 41